Spirits Distilled

Stories and Memories Of
The Upper Midwest

Jack Ozegovic

with Steve Semken

A Regionalist Publication
The Ice Cube Press
North Liberty, Iowa

Northern Spirits Distilled:
Stories and Memories of the Upper Midwest

©Copyright 2000 Jack Ozegovic
with Steve Semken

First Edition
2 4 6 8 9 7 5 3 1

ISBN 1-888160-53-5

The Ice Cube Press
205 North Front Street
North Liberty, Iowa 52317-9302
E-mail: icecube@inav.net
Http://soli.inav.net/~icecube
Comments, questions and orders welcome

Library of Congress Cataloging Number
99-071800

Manufactured in the United States of America

Printed on acid-free, recycled paper
meeting library standards

Cover painting *River Scene* by Jack Ozegovic
Author photo by Ann Carlin Ozegovic

DEDICATION

I wish to dedicate this book to my wife, Ann,
in thanks for her help and patience which were
instrumental in bringing this effort to
conclusion, as well as to the memories of
David R. Fisher and Glendon Collier.

CONTENTS

ACKNOWLEDGMENTS

The author wishes to express his great indebtedness to the following for their assistance.

For technical advice and aesthetic guidance: John Clarke, Craig Lesley, William Pitt Root, Pamela Uschuck and David Vermetten.

For critical reading: Jerry Gates, Denise Low, Vic Herman, Paul Ingram, Laura Quackenbush, Shelly Maxwell, Tony Winter, Pauline Tyer, Laura Waldo-Semken.

For contributions of story detail, depth and local legend: Howard Crisp, Roger Gilroy, John P. Kelley, Richard Kline, Clif McChesney, Karen McDonnell, Janis Weaner, David and John Williams, Sarah and Ann Wunsch.

To Rosemary Virgo, who for many years has urged me to write something. And finally to Steve Semken and the Ice Cube Press for publishing what I eventually did write, not to mention the Ice Cube's perpetual guidance counselor Wendell the Wonder Cat.

INTRODUCTION

I first met Jack Ozegovic at an art opening in Lawrence, Kansas during the very early 90's. Not being an artist myself I often let my mind wander at these openings since I didn't understand what went into making art. I certainly didn't feel adequately informed to speak with anyone about theory, techiniques, or the history of art. Out of the blue I found myself standing next to a large man with a beard and a glass of wine in his hand. I immediately remembered having spotted this man at an opening a few months earlier. I had observed that he usually ended up talking to some of the more unusual looking people at the openings and for the most part he seemed to relish conversation, laughter and inspiration the artwork on display seemed to provide, rather than close theoretical examination.

I attended most of the local openings with my wife, a local artist, and her friends. I was usually ready to leave after a couple walks through the gallery. When I did speak it was always in a quiet and polite manner to some of her friends, or previous University instructors if they were in attendance. I didn't feel it was appropriate for me to talk about camping, compost, or fly fishing. For the most part I tried not to offend anyone as my perception of artists was that they were quite temperamental about their work. On this one particular evening, however, I found myself standing in front of a large porcelain bowl which to me looked like an oversized cowboy hat. I commented to the older gentleman next to me that maybe this was a tribute of some sort to John Wayne.

The man standing next to me began to laugh wholeheartedly. "Faaantastic! It does look like some sort of strange cowboy hat doesn't it! John Wayne would be proud I'm certain!"

I was very pleased to have received such a positive uproar on behalf of my comment. At this point the man introduced himself as Jack Ozegovic. I hoped that I might have an opportunity to began striking up a friendship with this older man, maybe even be included in his group of jovial buddies.

At future art openings and receptions I began to search for Jack as he seemed to have what I considered a good-hearted, open minded and authentic, as well as honest approach to art. Over time, as I talked to him at openings I began to inquire as to his whereabouts and background. When he began to relate his adventures in northern Michigan and his opinions regarding life I was continually in agreement and found myself laughing at the zany people he seemed to have discovered in this world. I had never met anyone who seemed to appreciate the values of individuality and honesty like he did. I knew

I had discovered a person who had a knack for locating interesting people and ideas. Someone able to inspire others, including me, to follow our dreams, to live as honestly as we wished and to snub the tyrannical Big Brother, government/corporate system.

What still amazes me is that Jack continues to find honest and creative people wherever he goes. In Lawrence, at one of his parties the house is always full of spirited people, not so much dreamers as individuals living the life of their choice. Not posers, or folks wrapped up in political correctness, but people who have original ideas.

Just last year I visited Lawrence and was happy to find Jack heading a table of morning coffee drinkers at the local food co-op. Everyone at the table was laughing and carrying on about the things in life that matter: creativity, stories, hopes, food, strange Aunts and Uncles, spirits and friendship. It so happened that I had brought along some of the traditional Plum Bounce Jack first discovered how to make in Michigan and which I now make with a variety of wild Iowa plums. Then, as any good group of people ought to do when presented with a gift, samples were passed around the table of nearly 15 people and everyone was able to share this Michigan recipe. Proving, in at least one way, that the life described in this book is still very much alive and being enjoyed.

I think that what tests a person most in life is change and dealing with the variety of unavoidable circumstances that each of us have to face. Things like moving and retiring; the deaths of loved ones, or changing occupations. What defines a person is if they continue to excel wherever they go. Can they maintain what they claim to stand for? In my opinion Jack has. He may not be in Michigan anymore, but he is still doing what he does best: exploring, discovering and inspiring the unique and creative traits that make up human nature.

Long Live Northern Spirits!
Steve Semken

Author's Prologue

The stories contained here are inspired by experiences during the twenty years I lived in northwestern, lower Michigan. They describe people and places I feel were integral parts of a rural sub-culture that was distinctive of the region.

This book has been written at the urging of friends in order to record certain aspects of this regional life-style. The people in the stories and the unique landscape are both rapidly vanishing. This was one of the reasons which motivated me to leave the area.

Our society has become increasingly mobile and wealthy during the past thirty years. The new communication technology gives people the option to leave large urban areas for a more pristine and quiet area without interrupting their livelihood. They search for smaller communities where schools are safer for their children, the life-style less frantic, where there is a cleaner and more beautiful environment, or all of the above. This mobility phenomenon and financial flexibility has affected the quality of life in many rural areas of the country since the early 1980's. I have observed this in parts of

Arizona, New Mexico, Colorado and Pennsylvania. Northern Michigan has not escaped this new migration.

When these migrations occur they can result in the upsetting of the cultural balance of a given area. The newcomers, while claiming to search for a more tranquil life, can actually transport with them the aggressive and arrogant actions they claim to be retreating from. They help create clogged streets, often adding to the preponderance of more aggressive driving habits. With the advantage of great wealth, they can also inflate local real estate values, creating pricy homes which the native resident can not afford. I observed in our township a wealthy newcomer demanding protection from the rural volunteer fire department. He wanted the services but it was beneath his dignity to turn around and volunteer himself.

New arrivals often did not share the values of being an old fashioned neighbor. Being a good neighbor was highly cherished in rural communities at one time but is now vanishing as many newcomers prefer to remain anonymous. I consider this to be a great loss to American society—the neighbor who cares and is there when you need help. These new migrants wherever they go, just by their numbers, destroy the very thing they claim to be searching for.

Another situation that contributed to the upheaval of social patterns in northern Michigan was the seesaw nature of the fresh fruit market. With increasing instability in the market, smaller growers found themselves against the wall. Then, with the emergence of global economy/marketing, the World Trade Organization and various other trade agreements, foreign produce, such as cheap apple juice concentrate from China, began to compete with the local grower. If a small grower wished to retire he may have trouble finding a family member to assume control of the orchard. Many of these people loved their land and the act of planting something on it. It was an act of bonding with the area, but they were prevented from continuing because of what some call progress. That word has always had connotations of change, but I always thought that this idea also entailed improvement. I see very little improvement except the filling of developers' pockets.

This book is my description of the good life my wife and I enjoyed in Michigan without being too sentimental. However, a certain sorrow emerges as I recall the dismembering of the serenity and freedom that once existed there along with the steady obliteration of an irreplaceable scenic landscape and prime fruit growing country. I do cling to many priceless memories and attempt to share a few of them here.

CHAPTER ONE
STARTING OUT

The northwestern lower peninsula of Michigan the way I know it is a land and time which will never be possible again. When I lived in Michigan I often wondered if I was behaving as a grown man was supposed to. Many times during a moment of jubilation I'd ask myself if what I was doing was really my life. Yet even as I thought these things, even as I questioned what was happening, I would find myself floating and taking off on another adventure, rollicking along with a carload of friends to visit some somber, nearly abandoned village like Stanleyville, or taking off to attend a local artists' party and an evening full of laughter, jest, drink and hilarity. At other times I would be out walking and exploring the vast and vacant open country side, able to feel free and at ease with the world. Like anyone, I never believed my life or the place I lived would change.

My years in Michigan were times of great accomplishment. I found that fun and pleasure could be mixed with personal integrity and community pride. Being who you needed to be didn't mean having to be staunch, bored, repressed, or politically correct. It was a time when being yourself without compromise was admired and rewarded, encouraged, even expected. There were no masks needed for the brave, and I was glad to call myself one of the brave. I was able to fulfill a version of the great American dream in a land and place that seems to be getting harder and harder to locate as the years go by. Individuality in this nation is drifting away like waves eroding the shores of Lake Michigan.

These free and heroic years of mine began in a remote region near the shore of one of our Great Lakes in northern Michigan. I can still remember my first autumn in 1968. There were high, billowy clouds drifting over my head. Light clouds floating in easy, simple, abundant and creative patterns just like me. I remember looking up and being anxious to rekindle my spirit, which had taken an unfortunate beating back East in the more pompous and formality driven region of the United States. That autumn day I had breathed deeply and discovered I was going to be able to roam the open landscape and live the way I'd always hoped.

The small town where I arrived was Chippewa Harbor, about fifteen thousand people in the northwest, lower part of Michigan, a little more than two hundred and fifty miles from the urban mass of Detroit.

As a young child I had visited this area with my family on summer trips. I carried a lingering memory of rolling hills, fallow fields and rows of silent Lombardy poplars along little-used railroad tracks. When I returned to begin my new teaching job I was pleased to find that things were still the way I'd remembered. The land would nurture my hopes and dreams.

The region was almost entirely inhabited by people born and raised there. Only occasionally did someone move in from the outside, and if so, they arrived to fill a particular need or skill that the town didn't already have. The area was quite removed from major highways, which made commercial shipping slow and expensive. This also seemed to inhibit rapid growth in population and industry. As a result, the town was able to maintain an independent life of its own. I found two primary industries when I arrived:

fruit growing and fruit canning. There was also, although very dormant at the time, a tourist industry. When I arrived the tourists were summer-long residents who owned homes in the area and returned summer after summer. It wasn't until later that this aspect of the town began to accelerate and explode.

I had jumped at the chance to move to Chippewa Harbor. Not that I had a choice, since I had been denied tenure at my last teaching job in Pennsylvania. The reason given was that neither my training nor my attitude was compatible with the direction that the college was taking, nor with the academic structure of the art department. I was desperately in need of a fresh start. Plus, I'd had enough of the whole self-important, presumptuous, Eastern life-style. They were right. I was not compatible, but at the time I didn't understand that.

My search for employment involved sending out letters to those I knew and to those I hoped might hire me. Thankfully I was invited to bring my teaching skills to northern Michigan. A former colleague in graduate school had become the chairman of the art department at Tamarack College in Chippewa Harbor and was eager to bring me aboard.

This job would prove to be a perfect match. The school itself was still new, but through the jitters of first opening and was slowly taking on the rewards of a permanent campus in town, such as satisfied students, a new basketball team to cheer and a variety of other school sponsored events, including faculty and guest artist openings. When I arrived, I was walking into a place that was prospering and growing, yet still open to new ideas. I found the art faculty and administration anxious and eager to work. They were excited about the future of education and the visual arts. The town, the land and the school seemed truly without limits.

I was eager to get out in the beautiful, open countryside. As a landscape artist I was overjoyed to find that I would be able to roam and explore the area without being bothered, or bothering others. The land was not posted and at most there may have been a few duck hunters meandering through the hills every so often, always visible of course, dressed in their blaze orange clothing. Wandering around during those early and comforting days I was able to revel in my drawing and painting with a satisfaction that I had rarely felt before, or since.

At first glance the countryside looked as pure and full of calm as the clouds overhead. Closer inspection, however, revealed numerous rotting stumps in the forest that were stark reminders of the devastation that occurred during the timber cutting era in the late nineteenth century. I also observed numerous, silent monuments to failed dreams in the varied shapes of abandoned farmhouses. All results of sorry and failed attempts to farm and live off the region's tricky, sandy soil. I would often catch a glimpse of an old lilac in bloom, or an isolated rose bush next to the rotting heap of a fallen down home. When I arrived it was only those who had understood the limits of sandy soil who were able to survive, and they did so by growing fruit, primarily cherries, and certain varieties of apples.

A perfect example of the boom and bust mentality was an area about fifteen miles west of town, which was reputed to be extraordinarily poor. It had been settled by small, independent and, of course, hopeful farmers who bought the land very cheaply after the lumber barons finished pillaging the forests. That land, however, was only marginally suited for farming. There were local stories of families roaming the woods in desperation in the early spring after their meager winter supplies had been depleted. Men hunting out of season; women and children scouring the woods for anything that could be put to use as food: mushrooms, fern sprouts, wild leeks, dandelions, or nettles.

Driving through this area was always a sad experience for me. I couldn't help but view it as haunted. In the late afternoon one's imagination could easily run away with ghostly images of past residents.

By the late 1930's, I was told, just about everyone had given up and left. The few that remained took on others' bad fortunes by obtaining more land and keeping small herds of beef cattle, or flocks of chickens for local sale and consumption. Those farmers stayed on, and those who dared to look bad luck in the face maintained a fierce independence from townspeople.

What the remaining farmers didn't use from the abandoned buildings was torn down by the old Michigan Forestry Department, or left to collapse into melancholy heaps of bricks, weathered boards and rafters under the weight of many winters. At the crossroads of this poor region all that remained were a crumbling concrete foundation of the general store and a small flight of stone steps leading nowhere. By the time I arrived the forest had reclaimed large portions of the gnarled little orchards and weed-choked vegetable gardens.

Another issue of local survival became obvious to me during my first few months in this northern town, and that was the role winter would play. The first year I moved in it was a record-setting winter. Snow fell twenty-four straight days and even made national news. It wasn't a steady snow, but snow fell in lesser and greater amounts the entire twenty-four days. My friends back in Pennsylvania could hardly contain their laughter, asking if I had set out for the Arctic Circle, wondering how my team of sled dogs was holding up. Of course I found the whole episode exhilarating. It was a true thrill to be around so much snow.

One of the highlights of that first winter happened on a clear, cold Sunday in January when I was suddenly inspired to try and find a suitable spot for ice skating. I spotted a place where numerous ice fishermen had parked and, to my great joy, noticed that the wind had blown the snow off a vast patch of frozen lake, revealing a smooth, deep layer of ice. I stumbled and lurched down through snow drifts, which were nearly as tall as myself, to the icy lake's edge. Sitting on a big, bumpy log, I adhered my ice skates to my feet, struggled through more snow and frozen sand until I reached the wind swept ice. Once secure upon the smooth ice, a rushing, uplifting spirit took over me. I had never encountered so much space to skate. Out on the middle of the bay, away from land I knew I made a good decision to come up here. I skated across and around the ice, staring off in all directions until it was well past dark. I waved at a passing ice fisherman and yelled to the world. There seemed to be no boundaries, no end to where I had just moved. I believed that my new home was the land of unlimited excitement and freedom. At the time I arrived, I believe I was right.

Just like the feeling out on the ice, the town itself was also open, free and independent when I arrived. There were no phony cocktail parties or thundering traffic noises. I didn't encounter the language of urban mass thinking—that pointless way of living, always full of critical and petty nit piking.

Eccentric qualities were valued and respected where I had moved. Exuding around me was a truly local subculture. A place all its own. The northern woods, it became apparent to me, was a community busy cultivating a unique type of people, many of whom I soon became attached to.

By the time I finally quit ice skating that winter day so long ago, the years of uncomfortable employment and nagging wishes to be close to nature had disappeared. I knew that at long last I was going to be able to pursue my own directions in sport and art and life.

CHAPTER TWO
MY HEROIC LANDLORD

One of the earliest personal encounters I had with local inhabitants was my first landlord, whom I and others affectionately called, "My heroic landlord." His name was Abe, and his life was a shambles. His path in life, it seemed, was lit by a blue flame of alcohol. Abe was constantly getting into trouble or screwing up. Yet what always amazed me was the joy and the pride he took in his failures. He never seemed ashamed of himself. Rather, he preferred to boast and show off his broad, proud smile in triumph. His behavior was so removed from time that his memory lingers with me to this day.

I was introduced to Abe almost immediately after I arrived in Chippewa Harbor. While looking for a place to stay one of the potters in the art department at the college recommended the apartment above Abe's house. Upon looking at the place, which was still being remodeled, it was agreed, between myself and the others, that I would stay in the apartment as soon as the remodeling was complete. I knew that rental property was hard to come by so took what I could get.

After a long delay in the remodeling process I finally moved in, having volunteered to finish painting the rooms myself in order to speed things up. After moving in I quickly realized the careless manner in which the apartment had been constructed. At the very best Abe had merely jerryrigged things together. The gas space heater had been stuck haphazardly between two walls in such a way that I feared the apartment might catch on fire during the winter. In fact, I was frightened to run the heater when I was asleep. He had done the same type of thing with the hot water heater, which was hidden, grumbling and moaning in the back attic area.

Living in an apartment maintained and arranged by my heroic landlord was terrifying. As for the furnishings that had been provided, nothing matched. I was always undecided as to whether the mattress was dangerous, ready to fall apart, or just painfully lumpy. Even the bathtub was poorly located. The tub had been shoved in the far corner of the bathroom, in such a way that because of the pitch of the ceiling I had to more or less lean forward and slide in. Then I would need to roll back out like some sort of arctic seal.

It wasn't long before I began to get an insight into this landlord and his personal living conditions. When I took my rent payment downstairs for the first time I discovered a life of pure and simple disaster. Entering his living room was worse than a junk yard. Everything he owned was mixed together. There were mounds and mounds of tattered and grubby clutter that all seemed molded together with an adhesive of dust and spider webs. Literally, there were heaps and piles of junk perched everywhere. There were morsels of uneaten food adorning several days of unwashed dishes. Careless living was obviously his familiar pattern. I thought it looked as though the Turkish Calvary had charged through his house. Any conception I had of what it meant to be sloppy was clearly visible. After wading through this mess, month after month, what began to dawn on me was that although he lived in total and utter disorder, he did so in good humor and even with a feeling of achievement.

Probably my first viewing of his famous, gleaming grin of misfortune—a grin which I soon learned preceded a string of disasters—was when he suspended an antenna wire for his ham radio. One Saturday morning, on my way downtown, I waved at Abe as he stood on his front lawn, a bundle of cable by his feet and a slightly befuddled look on his face.

When I returned after six, maybe seven hours, Abe's look of confusion had switched to that of excitement. He declared, that after a full day of shooting his bow and arrow, he had finally hung his antenna-guy wire. He had attached the guy wire to one of his deer hunting arrows and intended to cascade the wire over the upper branches of a large maple tree in his yard. After an entire day of effort, he had finally done it. So, as I approached, there he stood, in poorly cut jean shorts, mismatched socks and a filthy shirt, surrounded by a heap of beer cans. His ordeal with the ham radio antenna was complete and he was beaming with messy integrity. I could only imagine the various curses uttered along the way as well as the variety of spots where the arrow could have landed. Not seeing any angry parents, ambulances or injured pets, I felt a certain amount of relief, and joy while I stood there listening to Abe explain the odyssey he had lived through during the day.

Another incident which brought on the appearance of his carefree smirk was near the beginning of my stay. Early one morning I was roused with what had become a great moment in his life.

He had come charging up the apartment stairs, frantic and excited, banging through the door at some ungodly, dark hour to announce his news. A friend of mine was staying with me and the two of us awoke to hear him declare, without hesitation, "JACK! I was arrested and had to spend the night in jail!"

His pronouncement possessed no shame, no guilt, none of the humiliation most people would associate with having to spend the night in jail after being pulled over for drunken driving. Instead, my heroic landlord interpreted this as an accomplishment. He was happy, it was a blue-ribbon moment in his life and he wanted to share this event immediately. In fact he seemed to feel that being in jail was precisely the sort of thing that ought to be shared and gloated over. He obviously thought that I would develop a great level of admiration for him now that he had spent the night in the slammer.

During the year and a half I stayed at his apartment Abe made many efforts to explain to me why he considered himself one of the world's great lovers. It became clear, quite soon, that in addition to having no guilt about drunk driving and spending time in jail he also had no shame in cheating on his wife. He thought that having affairs was the natural thing for a man to do. He was persistently eager to brag about his efforts to have a lover behind his wife's back. I was always uneasy at his distorted ideas and tales of love, but listened all the same. Whenever I listened to his tales I believed him though. I never questioned his honesty, as misdirected as it was.

One time, when he thought that his wife was having an affair behind his back he became quite irritated. To try and get proof of this unthinkable act, he patched together a slipshod tape recorder system of hidden microphones which he decided to headquarter in the small attic area behind my apartment. It was all quite concocted, as though a Rube Goldberg cartoon, and destined to be a failure. There were wires and holes going all over the house when he finally finished creating this elaborate spy system. He never did get any proof of his wife cheating on him, but he remained incensed at the possibility.

Abe often demonstrated a strong desire to become part of my group of friends. From time to time my artist friends looked upon Abe as a rather interesting fellow. In fact, many people in the arts gravitate toward unconventional personalities, because unusual people are looked upon as being original. Of course, there is also the existential view: that the unconventional personality is the antihero of the so-called "normal" folk. The unconventional person then becomes a hero to some in the creative field, because of the belief that the unconventional individual has chosen a direction outside the herd. It was for these sorts of reasons that some, in my group of friends, held a certain sympathy for Abe. However, just when we were on the verge of becoming closer to Abe, even perhaps his friend, he would commit some monumental blunder that would cause all of us to back off to a safer distance.

The last debacle I had to endure with Abe, while his tenant, occurred two nights before my wedding day. A large group of us had stayed out late that night until my friend, Harold Kinard, and his wife returned to my apartment with me. The reason escapes me now, but as we ascended the stairs that evening, Abe spotted us and called out for all of us to come down and have a drink with him. As he led us through his junk strewn, pigpen, living area, it was obvious that he had been involved in some sort of celebration of his own. His gait and slurred speech made him seem on the verge of passing out. He led us along, wanting to serve us some of his custom spiked egg nog.

He was dressed, at this late hour, in his trademark outfit: a combination of rumpled t-shirt, pock marked with the stains and efforts of his heroic day and a pair of sagging, ill fitting trousers. While trying to fill our glasses Abe began to spill egg nog on all of us. Then, quite oblivious to his rueful act of pouring egg nog, he proceeded to try and give a toast to my future happiness, all the while slurring his speech and sounding utterly idiotic. Throughout the whole series of sorry events he continued to bear his broad and stupid grin, completely ignorant of our frustrations and disappointment. It donned on me that he alone seemed capable of understanding his own hilarity.

As a result of my casual friendship with Abe, and perhaps from a reluctant sense of obligation, I invited Abe to our wedding reception. This event was held at the home of my department chairman, who had quite generously opened his door to our guests and family. Much to the surprise of many, Abe arrived clean-shaven, well scrubbed and dressed in a well-fitting sport jacket that even matched his pair of neatly pressed trousers. He really made a grand appearance. However, as his consumption of wine and beer increased, his good behavior evaporated. Since his wife had chosen to stay at home with their baby, Abe was soon emboldened by enough alcohol to begin making passes at several of my wife's single women friends. These women already knew about Abe and were able to merely roll their eyes in disgust at his rather bumbling advances. In spite of being rebuffed, Abe still dove right into the middle of the evening's celebrations and genuinely enjoyed himself.

Later than I would have liked, Abe finally prepared to leave. As a proper and fitting end to the evening Abe did not disappoint. On his way home he skidded around an icy corner and slammed his car into a fire hydrant. His blue path of alcohol burning bright as ever.

It was many years later when I saw Abe for the last time. He spied me out across a street in town. When he spotted me, he waved and trotted over. Up close he appeared tired and quite worn out. He also remarked to me, with a certain amount of confusion and remorse, concerning his wife, "My god she left me." Then added in a slow and wishful tone, "and I was just about ready to settle down."

As I think back over the actions of my heroic landlord I believe that to him his life was a series of simple celebrations. Although he was a heavy drinker he wasn't a mean, sullen or remorseful drunk. For that matter, he wasn't even a loud drunk. Rather, he seemed to drink to relax and celebrate his attempts at life. It wasn't long before I began to understand how drinking was part of life in the Northwoods. I found that people drank to be alive. The drinking habits in the area might have been influenced by the rich ethnic mixture of Poles, Czechs and Germans. Beer and whiskey were just part of the food chain.

CHAPTER THREE
SLADEK'S BOHEMIAN
GARDENS

One month into my new teaching job at the college I was told to keep an eye out for a bulletin that would announce the "SEMINAR." This bulletin, I was advised, would simply appear on the staff billboard. When I asked, with innocence, "What do you mean?" I was informed that the Dean of the Faculty lived above and led informal gatherings at a tavern on the west side of town called Sladek's Bohemian Gardens. I still remember to this day how I thought to myself, "Had I heard correctly? A college dean who not only lives above a tavern, but conducts gatherings there as well?" Well, in comparison with my earlier experiences at other schools, I believed I must have entered paradise. So I began, with great anticipation, to keep my eyes open for the announcement of the seminar. This, I knew, was not something I wanted to miss.

Finally the coveted notice was posted and I eagerly waited for Friday evening to arrive. At first I was looking forward to meeting and gathering with my colleagues. However, as soon as I saw it, what I quickly became just as excited about was the discovery of Sladek's Bohemian Gardens. It wasn't until years later that I was able to reflect back on how broadly the location of the Dean's seminars had affected me. In due time, Sladek's would indoctrinate me into a hub of comfortable, occasionally raucous, regional and authentic life.

My first visit to Sladek's was memorable indeed. Almost immediately my idea of entering paradise seemed to come true. The seminar itself was a comfortable enough evening spent with my fellow staff members, orchestrated by the Dean, as if he were a King. He conducted his royal court at a large, heavy wooden table at the rear of Sladek's. This back room had once been reserved for Indians only. He would often provide long and useful rants regarding the college, or local economy to all of us gathered around.

Sladek's was a long, solid, ponderous and very old wooden-framed building with a tall false-front facade. There was a cornerstone dating the structure back to 1882. It was said that the original Sladek family had devoted much of their own time and labor on weekends to erect this treasure. Over the years it had withstood lumberjack brawls when loggers would arrive in robust and wild fashion for weekend benders and festivities. Of course, there were also the glorious drinking and celebratory life-styles of the Czech migrants who had built and inhabited the building since the tavern's inception. A rough and tumble history was grandly visible to me as I approached the building for the first time. I knew that this building was a testament to the variety of emotions and actions which create real life.

The interior of the place possessed sixteen, perhaps eighteen-foot high ceilings which were still covered with decorative and original tin plating. The decor was appropriate for the Northwoods as the walls were lined with stuffed hunting trophies. There were heads of all kinds of animals hanging about: Elk, Moose, Deer, Bobcat, Beaver and Bear. There were also Ducks and Squirrels, Muskrats, large Brook Trout, Pheasants, even an illegal Bald Eagle that had been there so long the legal officials had simply turned their backs. Most of the animals seemed to have been prepared by an incompetent taxidermist since a significant number of the Deer and especially one of the Beavers had been rendered a glassy, cross-eyed, silly expression across its face. Later on when a new owner took over, a Deer's rump was hung with the joke that this was all any hunter attending Sladek's would probably be capable of glimpsing. Over time the walls acquired other items such as a Hammerhead Shark, which was worth a chuckle or two as it was supposedly on loan, yet as permanent as the tin ceiling. And, of course, there was also a Jack-A-Lope, the taxidermist joke of portraying a cross between a Deer and Rabbit.

The entire tavern was covered in a patina made up of the dust of ages. The very air was heavy with the aroma of conversation. The rich smell of wood emitted radiantly from the thick and massive cast iron stove burning in the back corner. On rainy, autumn days there were times when it seemed the animals on the walls would come to life. It was rumored that when a rather prominent Republican politician was visiting town the Elk head had fallen off the wall on to the back of the VIP's head, pushing his face into a bowl of chili.

As my eyes moved about the place during my first visit to Sladek's, I remember seeing a large, old, wooden bar with its inviting brass serving rail, behind which presided the caretaker of the whole monument, Henry Sladek. He was a melancholy-looking, third generation, heir to the tavern. One of my memorable first impressions was of the sales case and old cash register where Henry sat. In this case, Henry made available many items that a fellow might need during a night of misfortune, such as aspirin, pencils, shoe laces, moldering candy bars and I think some rather old and out of date breath mints, as well as a small cache of antacid tablets for the truly unfortunate soul whose stomach might become uneasy during a busy night of unity amongst his friends. As I recall, all of the items in the case were coated in a thick mugging of well aged and powdered debris.

Over time I got to know Henry and realized that he had a rather rye sense of humor. He operated a tight ship inside the bar and had posted signs all over the place stating the rules: No loitering, No dancing, No profanity, No raucous behavior ... . Strangely, for a bar owner, Henry was quite a man of conviction. He closed at six o'clock in the afternoon on Saturday since he felt a man ought to be home with his family by that hour. One could often see Henry slumped sideways, wearing an expression of noticeable glumness. He was a tall, gaunt man and even though his rather morose attitude seemed cantankerous at times, he was still a very well loved owner. At times one would feel a little pity for him as he seemed on the verge of a sort of sullen grotesqueness.

The twist of fate that seemed settled over Henry's head was the fact that he never wanted to be a bartender in the first place, certainly not a tavern owner.

Early in his life Henry wanted to be a doctor and even moved to Chicago to begin his studies. He had been permitted to leave for his studies only upon a few conditions set out by his father. The first condition was that he live with a relative and the second condition was that when he returned home periodically he would agree to smuggle supplies of grain alcohol with him from Chicago. Since this was during Prohibition, Henry's father had special needs for some of his clientele upstairs at Sladek's. This arrangement was fine with Henry and went on for quite awhile.

Before Henry had completed his medical studies, however, his father passed away. As the eldest, and only son in the family, it was with a strict sense of obligation and custom that Henry return home to take on the chores and responsibilities of the family business. So, although Henry had never wished to be a tavern owner, he had spent his entire life involved with alcohol.

The title of tavern owner didn't happen right away. He needed to wait out the years of prohibition. When he first took over, the business was, in formality, an ice cream parlor. The family had removed the bar rail, which made the bar a serving counter in the eyes of the law, and an Uncle began to supply the ice cream. All along, of course, the upstairs continued to serve alcohol to the wealthier and more prominent citizens of town. No harm ever came out of serving alcohol during prohibition for

Henry. Since Chippewa Harbor was hours from the major cities, enforcement of prohibition was casual.

When prohibition ended, Henry may have maintained Sladek's as an ice cream parlor. But the locals and his family pressured him to favor the wild and festive mood swings associated with owning a tavern.

Sladek's Bohemian Gardens was a true refuge for me during my time in town. With no outside noise, it was a center of lively conversation rather than a joint to watch television, or listen to loud music. One could drink large steins of beer, or eat food in the company of others and speak freely. Atmosphere, charm and excitement were entirely created by the patrons. We didn't rely on the scores of football games, or the music of the times for entertainment, or diversion. It was not a spot where everyone went, and thus, this tavern developed a local subculture of various and memorable characters and, in my mind, heroes.

As for the seminars, they continued to occur with regular fashion until the Dean's family pressured him into moving to a "real" house. Finally, due to the Dean's poor health and eventually his death, the seminars came to an end. Certainly, this man earned the most respect of any dean I had ever worked for.

CHAPTER FOUR
THE MAKING OF
A FOLK LEGEND

Like any good social institution that man cultivates, the Dean's seminars, sadly, came to an end. However, this didn't mean I discontinued my journeys to Sladek's. I had become quite fond of the friendly atmosphere inside the old tavern. Many of my colleagues had developed a camaraderie during the seminars and so continued to meet at the tavern. It was a rare and genuine spot in town where I felt comfortable. Not only was it a place where I felt good, but I and many others considered ourselves loyal and important patrons. In fact, we came to believe that we were necessary components to the tavern's operations.

A few years after the seminars ended, Henry sold Sladek's to a new owner. The purchase agreement did not allow for any decor, or building changes, so things remained more or less the same through what was to become a frustrating series of new owners. That is, until the wife of the third new owner came along. This lady decided that she wanted to develop a more genteel crowd. Although no damages could be made to the building's existing structure, on account of historical status, apparently this didn't cover additions to the building. Thus, the wife harangued her husband into building a Victorian porch on the south side of the tavern from which would be served fancy and expensive dinners. Before long the side porch began to take precedence over the regular and devoted clientele in the main cavity of the tavern. As a result of this addition, the cluster of regular neighborhood patrons, of which I proudly considered myself part, felt left out. Suddenly we were unimportant. It was as if we were no longer good enough. We felt betrayed. All of us believed we had earned and deserved respect, and not getting it, our patronage fell off, including mine.

Thus, as happens quite often in human life, something which had once seemed very important in the lives of many people became altered. We were all taken by surprise and turned quite bitter.

Fortunately, this change was a long time in coming. Prior to the appearance of the Victorian porch, I was able to live and expand my wisdom as a citizen in the community of Sladek's Bohemian Gardens.

In the absence of juke box music or television Sladek's provided a center for human conversation. I always believed that it was this simplicity and uniqueness inside Sladek's that attracted the people whom I came to respect and cherish. In all senses, the tavern was a social community.

As I envision the cast of characters in my mind again, the images remain clear: broad men with big moustaches, withered old farmers dangling cigar butts in their mouths, hospital employees with rolled up sleeves, all varieties of hats worn askew. The full and salty odor of good tavern food and frosted mugs of beer, followed by the wipe of a wrist across the mouth. I never have trouble recalling the image of a retired fruit packer sitting in the still, even light of Sladek's, taking stock of years spent with stained hands and hot work. I always made an effort to take my out-of-town guests to Sladek's when they visited and without fail, its unparalleled atmosphere would impress.

Soon after the seminars ended, a student of mine, Russell Vanderbeck, became a bartender at Sladek's. This proved to be a good turn of events since it put someone of power on our side down at the tavern. When there might be a large crowd, Russell made a point of serving us first, or if we stayed after closing time we might get to finish the nearly empty bottles of finer whiskeys and Scotch. When a visiting professor was brought by we were always served quite well, even getting our own bowl of hot cashews from the old fashioned nut carousel near the front of the tavern.

Russell was a very competent bartender. He was able to monitor and control the patrons with a comfortable and fair firmness, conversed easily with people and possessed an apparently never ending knowledge of mixed drinks. A person could have a good time under his attention, but anything that became out of control was quickly dealt with. Although not a menacing man in size, he did have a full powered directness. For instance, one evening when the bar was closing, a large and boisterous gentleman from out of town tried to take his pitcher of beer with him, saying he had paid for it and that it was his. Russell stood in the door frame, grabbed the pitcher of beer, dumped the beer on the man's boots and declared, "You can have your beer, sir, but the pitcher is ours."

Russell was a sort of young curmudgeon. A freethinker who was always open and friendly as long as things were going okay. As a former soldier in the Viet Nam war though, he could take care of business when necessary. This earned him the respect of many.

Perhaps the most memorable of all the Sladek characters was Arnie Kretschmer. Arnie arrived at some point during the early seventies and was always recognizable by his funny looking, Greek-style fisherman cap perched above his thin and somewhat sad looking face. Once Arnie arrived in town he wasted no time getting comfortable in Sladek's. Arnie quickly logged more hours at the bar stool than anyone else. It simply was not his custom to leave. In fact, he usually didn't leave by choice, but by being kicked out, or if not kicked, then dragged, a look of helpless pity cast from his frail body. He would always toss and roll his eyes in helplessness.

When being removed, Arnie always acted as if he had done nothing wrong and was being treated in an entirely unjust fashion. To an outsider his look, when being removed, would have seemed to say, "How could I, a meek and feeble old man ever do anything wrong?" Those of us who had learned to understand him, knew better.

One evening when Arnie was being exceptionally annoying to Russell and his helper, Pete Orslund, they hatched a plan to end Arnie's badgering and barbed comments for good or, at least, for the evening. Russell, armed with hammer and nails, told one of the waitresses to tend bar for a few minutes as he and Pete had a chore to do. Then, before an astonished crowd, Russell and Pete grabbed Arnie firmly under the arms and dragged him out the rear door. The whole time Arnie put up a mock and pathetic battle. He wound a foot under a table leg, held on to a radiator, kicked over chairs, even left clawing finger marks along the wall. Finally, Russell and Pete shoved Arnie out the front door, then promptly nailed the door closed. On the way back to the bar, Russell realized that Arnie, a chain smoker, might very likely set the place on fire and no one would be able to get out. The nails were quickly removed, but to everyone's relief, Arnie didn't return that night.

Arnie's slight build was normally covered in a combination of checkered pants, fancy striped shirts and mismatched neckties. Other fine details of Arnie's appearance included drops of dribbled soup, splashes of coffee, splatters of cream and a good collection of poorly placed cigar burns on the edges of his already ugly suit coat.

We all came to understand it wasn't dressing that Arnie excelled at. What he really specialized in was straight Vodka and an occasional ice cube. Over time we all became quite fond of Arnie. Later on he was to become the all-time hero of us all.

Arnie was an unlikely folk hero since on a normal day he was, at the very least, a cantankerous, badgering, sarcastic, barbing, pestering and insulting old man. He seemed to despise people generally. His bitter tongue was a good defense system, but an even better method of attacking others. Arnie possessed a quick and pointed wit. He was also seemingly well read in a diverse range of literature, which he used to enhance his stream of insults. He could and did jab at people so ruthlessly that it was amazing he never once had anyone physically harm him. It was the constant, sharp, slicing jeers which caused him to get kicked out of the bar on a regular basis. Watching Arnie, though, I noticed that he was never loud, never crass, or even crude. He simply had a quiet and persistent method of insulting and annoying people, somewhat like fine sand paper.

When Arnie got kicked out of the tavern, he didn't have far to go. Conveniently, Arnie lived just behind and two buildings down the alley from the tavern with his mother, Minnie. Arnie moved in with her following his retirement from the automobile industry in Detroit. His regular routine was to arrive around noon and sit down with his Vodka. Then, as his alcohol consumption would increase, Arnie would choose someone to pester until he got thrown out.

Minnie, an old farm mother, must have been quite oblivious to Arnie, or very used to his ornery attitudes. Yet, every once in a while she would show up in the tavern, a small black purse clutched under her arm, plastic curling irons all over her head, to tug Arnie by the ear, back home. Watching this eighty-year-old mother pull her sixty-year-old son home was always a stitch for all of us. We would hoot and holler with all our might as Minnie entered the tavern, shouting warnings at Arnie to take cover and hide. Then, in silence, we would all stare in dismay as Minnie yanked and pulled him from the tavern's premises. After Arnie was removed we would all, once again, break out laughing. Someday, we all joked, she would transform Arnie into a decent citizen.

Another incident of genuine amazement to us was when Russell Vanderbeck had been drinking with Arnie one afternoon after he got off work. After a few drinks, Arnie insisted that Russell come over to his home so that he could show off some kind of clever gadget he had invented. While in the kitchen, Arnie pulled out a pistol and pointed it above the refrigerator at some invisible, makeshift target, then began to blast off a few shots. Under the pressure and insistence of Arnie, Russell did the same thing, letting loose a few bullets into the wall.

On the way out, Russell noticed Minnie sitting in the next room, in a chair, next to a soft glowing light, completely calm. All of this quite upset Russell. He honestly felt that Minnie could have been killed. Arnie waved off the whole notion with a brash snuff out his nose. This left all of us wondering if this was the normal turn of events at Arnie's, or if his mother was just completely deaf.

Arnie was a genuine pain in the ass. For instance, one time someone, a tourist perhaps, came into Sladek's and ordered a hamburger. After ordering his burger, the man went to the rest room, and, in his absence, Arnie reached over and took a bite out of the man's food. Actually, he'd taken a rather large bite. When the man returned he simply looked appalled and flatly disgusted. He didn't stop to eat. Instead, he just calmly walked out of the tavern, not complaining at all.

While he was an unlikely hero if you'd seen him sitting there pestering people on his bar stool, Arnie's heroic moment came about because of a local testimonial dinner in town. The big dinner was planned in order to help a United States Republican Congressman recover his campaign debt following his loss in the latest election. It was a big moment for the Chamber and larger business people in town, exactly the types of people almost all of us at Sladek's despised. It was this event that laid the ground for Arnie's heroism.

What happened was that two younger Republicans in town, who hadn't appreciated being bullied into purchasing tickets for the big testimonial dinner, came by Sladek's and asked Russell who the most obnoxious person in the bar was and would that person like to attend the big event? Well, without blinking an eye, Russell and everyone else immediately pointed to Arnie and so it was done. Arnie was escorted by someone else in the bar to the Republican fundraiser.

Dressed, as only Arnie could, in an assortment of mismatched and tobacco stained clothes along with his fisherman's cap, Arnie walked out of Sladek's to the cackles and whoops of all of us. He was destined for glory. As Arnie and his chauffeur walked up and presented their tickets for the event, they certainly caused the doorman some reason for alarm. A ticket to this powerful dinner was not easy to come by and so the doorman really made a rather blundering mistake by letting Arnie in. However, since Arnie did have a ticket in his hand, the doorman had an obligation to let him enter.

Arnie sat down beside an aide to Mr. Howard Baker, one of the Republican bigwigs who was to speak during the evening. Well, as the aide was looking over the speech papers for Mr. Baker, Arnie belched out in a firm and haughty tone, "Stop rattling those papers! You're making me nervous. I'm trying to eat my dinner!" This loud quip was shortly followed by a steady stream of similar invectives.

As the evening went on, Arnie went out of his way to be a nuisance. He would speak out at inappropriate times, yelling in disagreement with the speakers, clapping at numerous wrong moments and causing great embarrassment for the town's hot shot organizers. Finally, those in charge of the big event got fed up with Arnie's actions and ushered him out of the dining hall. Arnie went out as he often did when being kicked out of Sladek's, looking helpless, as if a victim, not like the ill-mannered fellow that he was. Then, with all eyes on him, nearing his way out the door, still uttering a continuous stream of pestering, ill-mannered and inappropriate comments at machine gun-like speed, Arnie paused, shook his arms free of the men guiding him out, raised his arms in protest and shouted, "No Pictures!"

Meanwhile, back at Sladek's a large crowd had gathered as the news about Arnie attending the testimonial dinner spread. We were all in a frenzy, waiting to hear of the mess we knew he would certainly create. Many, in fact most of us, had stayed much later than usual awaiting his return. Finally, as he walked through the door, a chorus of loud and rousing cheers took place, all of us admiring Arnie, who lightly bowed and swiftly moved back to the counter where he resumed his customary bar stool in front of a waiting glass of vodka, presented to him by Russell.

The escort who had accompanied Arnie recounted the events of the evening, which brought on more series of gurgling cheer. We all stood, doubled over in laughter and glee at the horror that must have been on the faces of the town's big shot Republicans. In rare fashion, Arnie had fulfilled half the town's dreams. It was this event that transformed Arnie from local town drunk and blathering gadfly, into an admired and respected folk hero.

We found out later that the two men that gave away the tickets were caught and severely reprimanded by their employers for their part in the prank. However, no one could ever take away the fame and prestige that had been laid upon Arnie that evening. He had single-handedly ruined the event. The local Republicans were branded as fools.

CHAPTER FIVE
AN ECCENTRIC REFUGE

Certain types of people migrated to the area of northern Michigan because the remoteness appealed to them. As a rather silent and isolated area, many unique and eccentric characters felt right at home. We didn't welcome these people to the area in order to laugh at them, or to mock their differences, rather, their devotion to individuality was respected and even envied from time to time.

The initial group of migrants that came to my attention, and who interested me with their shrouded mystique and phantomlike qualities, were the Stanleyville Intellectuals. For many years I only heard about, but was never able to meet them. They were so-named because the group rented and began to purchase haunted, ramshackle farm houses near the old town of Stanleyville. This town had originally been no more than a weak clustering of sad, rundown houses even in its meek heyday. We all claimed the town had been inhabited by a strange race of rather bleak and mutant derelicts.

For the most part the Intellectuals were dropouts from Southern Michigan University. Not high school dropouts, but graduate school, doctorate program dropouts, most of whom had been majoring in Liberal Arts programs such as English literature.

Their mysterious, and rumored intelligence began to create a local lore. Many of us began to whisper about them in a sort of mythical way behind their backs. The cluster of Intellectuals was in tune with many people of the time. All across the whole country during the sixties and seventies younger people were in search of a simpler, or in their minds, "purer" life-style. People wanted to experience some sort of close and spiritual connection with the land. The Stanleyville Intellectuals presence also acted as a magnet for other disenchanted people passing through, such as roving folk musicians, who it seemed, in the seventies, were constantly journeying through the area like medieval minstrels. I always felt that the saddened and disenchanted area these intellectuals had picked for themselves to inhabit was perfect since Stanleyville was such an isolated and distant old town itself. Appropriate for singing and thinking about the array of changes around us all.

When, upon occasion, any of us in town, or at the college, might meet one of these intellectuals they were quite interesting, but extremely eccentric. Unfortunately they were almost always too peculiar to befriend. They all seemed to have become too disaffected and guarded against everyday life.

It was never certain to me, or my friends, just how many of these intellectuals there were. Our guess was anywhere from seven to twenty-five. As time passed the group added to the region's rather weird qualities, especially since many of these transplants worked part-time in town, doing various tasks such as carpentry and small dairy farming chores. Then, when they had a sufficient supply of money put aside, they would disappear in order to write and study.

When I first became aware of these phantom intellectuals, my friend Harold Kinard and I made a quest to what we had heard was their headquarters, an old lounge at the decrepit Stanleyville Hotel. Like bird watchers, we hoped to get a glimpse of an intellectual. When we arrived at the old hotel lounge the environment was certainly not one of stirring, lively, intoxicating inspiration. In fact, the hotel was drab, stood two crooked stories high, and, to tell the truth, felt rather seedy with all its spider webs and a small cluster of tacky green coffee mugs stacked on a shelf. It certainly was not an impressive headquarters for a clan of superior geniuses, such as the intellectuals were considered to be.

The hotel tavern was actually clean enough, it just lacked any real charm. The floor was covered in funny looking, yellow linoleum, and the furniture consisted of spindly wooden chairs and frail tables. The walls were noticeably vacant and bland. We sat there a couple hours, nursing beers at the bar, waiting in vain for an enlightened intellectual to appear, but none did.

There were times when my friend Bandy McPherson, a member of the English department, would fill me in with what he felt were exciting stories of the intellectuals. Many of his stories involved the intellectuals partaking in long, nearly deadly, drunken weekends in the company of a local and nationally known poet. They were clinging to the hope that fame might blow their way perhaps.

Often, when a visiting poet or writer would appear at the college, Bandy would point out the Stanleyville Intellectuals in the crowd. Whenever they would appear in the crowd, my curiosity would get the better of me as I peeked views of them across a room. I was truly enchanted with their aura and wanted to understand and know them better. I am not sure what I expected, but usually when I got to see one of them, they appeared rather dingy, morose and even depressed. Not at all like the mythical creatures I expected them to appear as. When spotting them I would wonder why Bandy spoke of them with such dreamy-eyed respect.

I would question his declarations–did they really merit attention and respect as intellectuals, or were they simply incapable of dealing with the more structured and social world of academics they had left behind? Were they simply not good enough to get graduate degrees? What I believe intrigued all of us most was a secret admiration we had for the intellectuals and their decision to leave behind a safe and traditional life-style in academics to follow an alternative course of their own.

However, over time the group of intellectuals faded away. By the end of the seventies we would hear about how one or another of them had drifted off with a friend, a new wife, or just run out of money and gone back to Southern Michigan University. After ten years of mystery they had been all but forgotten.

For a brief time I was able to strike up a rather limited friendship with one of the last of the intellectuals. This lingering Stanleyville Intellectual introduced himself as Lewis Clamper. I discovered that his quest was to restore an old lake steamer back to its original working condition. At one time he had been a promising student of middle English literature. Unfortunately Lewis was quite difficult to engage with. He was very guarded and suspicious of me, not very open about himself, and boorishly silent on stories surrounding the group of intellectuals. I finally got tired of his extreme and suspicious eccentricity. My desire to get to know one of the Stanleyville Intellectuals ended in rather flat disappointment.

Another story of migrant life was what I called the house of disaster. This story revolved around an early migrant to the area, Arthur Clabberstein. Arthur appeared on the scene a few years before I did. His family owned a great holding of pristine and prestigious land, near a beautiful inland lake a few miles outside Chippewa Harbor. A simpler, perhaps saner man than Arthur might reasonably have been satisfied on this tract of land for eighty lifetimes.

Arthur was a graduate of Cambridge University, and after his graduation he was hired to teach Philosophy at the college. A very rich man, in fact the eventual heir to a large Midwestern grocery store chain, teaching Philosophy at the school soon proved to be more than Arthur was capable of doing. His life of luxury had not prepared him for the rigorous, never-ending series of organizational tasks and variety of social obligations that being a teacher required.

After a few years of merely taking students, and often whole classes, out to dinner and breakfast rather than teaching them, Arthur was asked to look for a new vocation. Since money wasn't really an obstacle for Arthur this news didn't upset him as much as it might others when losing their jobs. He had simply been involved with the school as a sort of recreational pastime.

After he was released from the school, Arthur decided to build a new home for himself along the clear and beautiful lake his family owned. This avocation proved to be a Herculian task for Arthur as well. In the course of his efforts to construct this new house he drove his hired help insane.

Arthur spent years changing his quirky mind about the tasks and projects for the new house. Early on, Arthur hired a private builder that would remain employed for ten, maybe as long as fifteen years. We all felt pity for this humble and dutiful man since Arthur's ideas of building were entirely spontaneous and bumbling, not in tune with what engineering and construction required.

Another major obstacle was that Arthur had no conception of what hard, manual labor entailed. He wasn't necessarily mean-spirited, he just didn't understand the blood and sweat someone needed to exude in order to accomplish tasks. Arthur requested continually that things be rebuilt, altered, or replaced.

The builder he had hired, Fergus Broadwelt, followed Arthur's loony requests for years. He felt an obligation and duty to satisfy his client's wishes, as would any honorable employee. Loyalty allowed the house to remain in a state of constant reconstruction. Fergus would come in to Sladek's with his friends and family, explaining the variety of changes that Arthur had requested. Fergus' family and close friends would always sit with mouths agape: sizes of doorways were changed, windows moved, even whole staircases taken apart and relocated. The more we heard, the more we realized, there was almost no chance the house would ever be completed. We all became quite disgusted with the indecision of Arthur.

As the years dragged on, Fergus finally got to the point where he could no longer stomach Arthur's impulsive requests. The final blow occurred when a heavy, stone fireplace was nearing completion and Arthur suddenly declared that he didn't like the position it was in and wanted the whole thing moved two feet to the left. At this point Fergus could handle no more. He had been silent and withstood many years of frustration over Arthur's quirkiness, but at this insistence he threw up his arms in despair and quit on the spot, driving off in his pickup truck, shaking his head in disbelief, yelling out at Arthur that he was a nut case!

Arthur did appear in town upon occasion. He would book an expensive room at the local hotel for a weekend and from time to time he even showed up at Sladek's.

Arthur was actually quite an attractive man, tall, with a square jaw and a soft, athletic build. He would walk in to the bar, see someone he knew, buy them a drink, then out of impulse buy everyone in the bar a drink. Yet he was consistently mysterious, and would never really talk to anyone for any length of time. For instance, after buying everyone a drink at the bar, he would simply disappear. I often wondered about his attention span. His continuously impulsive actions and mysterious appearances, as well as disappearances, established him as a full-fledged local eccentric.

For a short time, while in his mid-forties, although I never knew his exact age, Arthur made a short-lived attempt at being a married man. He had found a recent and refined divorcee, who frequented many of the same local artistic events as he. She had also come from a rather wealthy family and hoped that Arthur might continue to provide her with the upper class life-style to which she and her two children were accustomed to.

Unfortunately, as was always the case with Arthur, he was unable to carry out this partnership, not to mention that he was sorely inept at relating to the children. In fact, it was said that Arthur was barely even able to behave amicably toward the children. The marriage lasted a mere eight months, and ended rather bitterly. Arthur's curious life-style interested many, but his inability to relate to others for any length of time kept him isolated.

The last time I remember seeing Arthur was about a year before I left town. It was at a local art opening. With his usual spontaneity he had asked several of us to go out country-western dancing with him, which we did. Then, just as we were all in a circle, preparing to dance, we noticed that Arthur had once again disappeared, this time forever. I've never seen him again.

I often think of Arthur. I wonder if his house was ever completed. I wonder if he is out wandering the streets aimlessly at night by himself. Perhaps he is buying a round of drinks for a roomful of strangers.

CHAPTER SIX
THE VINEYARD SAGE

Perhaps the most memorable and widely known of the migrants to Chippewa Harbor was Ernie Bickel. I was introduced to Ernie after my first faculty meeting in the fall. Following the closing words of the college president, my chairman and I slowly walked through the stately pine trees that filled the center commons of the college and ventured into the library, where I was told of the fellow named

Ernie, the head librarian. I was told that Ernie would be of great assistance to me as I put together material for the art history classes I was to begin teaching.

As we entered the main door of the library, the newest building on campus, we swung a hard right into the administrative section and headed on through to the head librarian's office. Being a prisoner of stereotypes, I expected to find an orderly and well tended office area. To my utter surprise the room was piled randomly with books, periodicals, stacks of paper leaning at dangerous angles, many picturesque calenders and an assortment of small arctic animal carvings, which I later learned were Ernie's personal collection of Eskimo art. Behind this clutter, seated at an old desk, was not a neat, bureaucratic looking man in dark suit and red tie, but a sort of rumpled fellow in a plaid shirt and baggy trousers, leaning back in a swivel chair, not looking very alert at all.

After some introductory words and a few chuckles, my chairman left to tend to other business, leaving me alone with Ernie. After a few groans and wheezes, a brief comment about the honor of stoics, he said to me, "So, we have another artist to deal with." Then, he straightened up in his chair and began telling me about the library collection and how to search for needed books. We took a walk through the book shelves and Ernie pointed out the areas where I could find what I was looking for. On the way back to his office, he led me through the work area, where several women were cataloging, or preparing new books for the shelves. This area seemed as casual and as cluttered as Ernie's office. I felt very comfortable. The atmosphere was a complete contrast to the library at the college in Pennsylvania that I had just left. There, the librarian ran the facility with an iron hand. Everything was orderly and in its place, but the atmosphere was also sterile and prison-like. The library assistants had always scurried about like frightened rodents. It had always been hard to linger there and relax.

As autumn began to fade into winter, I found myself spending more time in the library, and also began to become more familiar with Ernie. After one research session, I stopped by his office late in the afternoon when his daily work would have been pretty much completed. Ernie was a man with a very sober expression and a sagging face. His sleepy looking face masked what was a constantly active mind. Upon first meeting this man, a person might think that this fellow was a rather sluggish and unengaging conversationalist, but that perception would soon be washed away. Ernie spoke in a slow, low tone and his expressions were rather laconic, yet his thoughts were neither trivial, nor his interests shallow and limited. He tied each word, each sentence together deliberately and individually, even stressing certain letters of important words. One sat hinged with anticipation, waiting eagerly for what he had to say.

I discovered that he was born on a farm in Indiana and had grown up with both a solid work ethic and a love for the land. My interest in landscape as a subject matter for much of my art work brought us closer, especially after I explained how I chose to interpret nature rather than copy it.

Sometime during the following spring, I mentioned to Ernie that I would be possibly driving around Benedict County on Saturday for a landscape photo run and that I'd like to stop at his place and visit for a while. He agreed. I found his place in the middle of the afternoon. As I pulled into the drive and parked, Ernie slowly emerged from the large old farmhouse that was his home. After some brief opening comments from each of us, he said that he wanted to give me a tour of his fifteen acres, so that he could show me his experimental vineyard and gardens. As we walked, he pointed out various grapevines and explained that they were French hybrids. He also told me of the fine qualities that each grape would reveal, as part of a blended wine, or as a singular vintage.

Along with this array of facts, he interjected stories of his own father's wine making, back during Prohibition. He told me how one time a rumor had reached them that revenue agents were going to hit their county in search of illegal alcoholic beverages. This demanded some immediate and decisive action, Ernie explained. He and his brothers were roused out of bed one cold autumn morning and the barrels of homemade wine in the cellar were hurriedly loaded on the old Ford truck and driven, on a circuitous route over little used back roads, into Indianapolis where they were quietly hidden in the cellar of a bakery owned by an Uncle. Two days later, the revenue agents appeared in a big black Buick, but found nothing in the cellar and left rather red faced.

As I walked along with Ernie, I noticed how well maintained his vineyard was and how neatly the garden plots were being prepared for spring planting. With five children to feed on a librarian's salary, the garden was most important. I mentioned to him how straight the support poles were in the vineyard and how tight the wires were stretched, yet I saw no one working. It was all so amazing, as if elves had done everything in a few minutes, then vanished up in smoke. Ernie explained how his five boys did most of the chores, adding, "I send them t' bed tired." He explained how he had taught them the value of work. His teachings had obviously taken effect. The place was immaculate. He told me, "A man cannot be at peace with himself unless he can dig in the dirt."

After this meandering walk on the slopes of his property, Ernie led me down a short flight of stone steps and through the outside cellar door to his special research room beneath his house. As we entered the narrow doorway, crouching because of the low ceiling, I made out about ten five-gallon glass carboys containing red and white wines. A makeshift bookshelf lined one wall and it was piled with three ring notebooks which, he explained, contained yearly records of rainfall, sunlight, average temperatures and soil sample results, as well as a summary of the wines for each year. His observations and records did, indeed, seem like magic.

We sat down on two apple crates and Ernie began uncorking various wines, pouring rather generous glasses of each. Most were without names as yet, bearing only numbers for identification. Each succeeding glass was a completely different flavor, full of unique taste and aroma. As we consumed glasses of different wines, Ernie slowly transformed into a loose tongued scholar. Waxing eloquent and waving his arms in dramatic gesture; making profound philosophical statements, richly augmented by his knowledge of renowned thinkers from Cicero to Ambrose Bierce. I was totally swept away by this man's depth of knowledge.

After several hours of this spellbinding discourse, I suddenly was aware of the time closing in on the dinner hour and I announced my departure, which was vigorously protested. Ernie walked slowly to the stairs, hollered to his wife and asked her if she could set an extra plate for dinner. The answer was affirmative and we carefully hoisted ourselves up the narrow steps, into the kitchen and emerged into the chaotic world of Claudia, Ernie's wife, as she prepared dinner for eight.

I had met Claudia briefly at college functions, but I had not seen her in her own element before. She was a smiling, rotund woman, who was totally outgoing, whereas Ernie was calculating and deliberate. She swiftly moved around the kitchen, seeming to do three things at once, as opposed to Ernie, who shuffled through one thing at a time.

We sat down to a mountainous spaghetti dinner and were joined by the five boys who ranged in age from fourteen to four. They were all energetic and alert, but also well behaved and courteous. Everyone ate with gusto. Ernie continued to be generous with the wine, which added more to the festive nature of things, but the wine was not there as a way to reach some different state of reality, but as a part of the euphoric celebration of being alive. I soon had to convey my thanks and depart before I became an unwilling overnight guest on the couch. While driving back to town I realized that I had discovered another paradise besides Sladek's Bohemian Gardens. How fortunate could a fellow get in this life.

Following this wonderful evening, I saw more of Ernie, but tried not to become a pest and ruin my welcome there. My next prolonged encounter with his supreme hospitality came a week before my marriage. I was informed that Ernie would host a stag party in my honor. It turned out that this was a tradition at the college, the tradition having started ever since Ernie's first significant grape harvest had been deemed fit for human consumption. Thus, a Friday night was selected and I was told to leave my car at home. Ernie would pick me up. Another part of the tradition was that the prospective groom was to be treated to dinner before the other celebrants arrived.

Upon arrival at the big farmhouse I once again found the usual chaos in the kitchen, full of the energy and tornadic action of Claudia and the five boys. Ernie led me to the next room, a large parlor, where he determined that a pre-dinner toast was in order. Much to my ecstatic joy, Ernie had procured a bottle of Slivovitz, the national libation of my father's native Croatia. This beverage is a distillate from a plum mash and of high alcohol content, able to warm one's total being like a kiss from Buddha. Several of these toasts were then followed by some fine wine. When Claudia finally announced that dinner was ready, we charted a crooked path into the kitchen indeed.

Nearing the end of dinner other cars began to arrive, containing many fellow faculty members, all in high spirits and looking forward to another of Ernie's Bacchanalias, as he had labeled these premarital gatherings. We were all served generous portions of Ernie's nectar from the basement and shortly thereafter the downstairs was cleared of wife and boys and the various games and loud conversation took over.

After hours of fun and games, Ernie yelled out, clinking a fork to the side of his glass, and captured the attention of the increasingly unruly bunch of men. He was standing in front of a large chalkboard, used for family messages, ready to give his lecture, which was commonly referred to by others as *Ernie's Guide To Marital Bliss*. With dramatic voice and gesture, Ernie began to address me on how to behave during my honeymoon night and, he assured me, if this advice was followed, I would be embraced with total and long lasting wedded bliss forever. His flowery lecture was bolstered with phrases and clumsy drawings of the female anatomy. This was as far as it went though. Ernie would have nothing to do with such things as crude movies during his Bacchanalias.

After about thirty minutes of earnest lecturing, Ernie turned to illustrate a point on the blackboard when suddenly he began to lurch backwards, falling into the laps of two guests. He had not let go of the chalk, which created a long, curving line across the length of the blackboard. A howl of laughter greeted Ernie as he sheepishly tried to regain his composure and resume his illustrated lecture. With an embarrassed smile, he quickly wrapped up his lecture, realizing that his endurance was rapidly waning. The period of revelry had come to an end. After all, the sun was only a few hours from rising.

I'm not sure who drove me home that night, but what does remain in the dim reaches of my memory is that, after weaving up the stairs to my apartment above Abe's, I stopped for a moment and looked out over the quiet, snow covered landscape around me. Though in a deplorable state, I was aware of having spent an evening of warm comradeship in the company of good men. I softly chuckled and thought how this never could have happened in Pennsylvania, then flopped off to bed.

In the spring of the following year there was another of Ernie's Bacchanalias to honor another colleague who was forsaking the single life. A few days after this event, however, Ernie announced that this was to be the last. He was, as we all were, disappointed, but he said that the faculty had become too large. Some of us also felt that many of the newer, and younger men didn't appreciate this type of folksiness anyway, even thinking it rather corny. Many of us consulted and believed that the priorities of the new generation were simply more devoted to themselves than the community. And so, just as I had watched the Dean's "Seminars" disappear, as well as nickel beer and the Passenger pigeon, so did I observe the passing of the Bacchanalia, another tragic loss for mankind.

Ernie did not disappear. In fact, the most monumental event in Ernie's life probably occurred about ten years after my arrival. He announced to me one day, in the faculty lounge, that he had been to the bank, received a loan and broken ground, at last, for the winery he had been dreaming of for so many years. He felt that his years and years of research and accumulated data were over and that it was time to take the next step. A cellar would be partially buried in the slope of a hill to insure a stable, year-round temperature. He was so excited, explaining how he intended to go about finding used equipment, presses, filtering devices, de-stemmers, and bottling equipment, as well as the giant fermentation tanks that would be needed. Everyone was very happy for Ernie, even, perhaps, a bit envious since here was a man, a rare man, who was seeing a long-held vision come to life. So few of us ever reach that plateau of satisfaction in our lives. His years of careful planning and wishful dreaming had finally produced results. We all agreed it couldn't have happened to a better guy.

Over the next ten years, following the beginning of his winery, things changed. Although Ernie was still seen in the library, the tasting room at his winery became his true living room. Most of his life, certainly his social life, was now conducted from there. Also, because the success of his product was becoming widely known, he became the pioneer of a new industry in the region. Several other wineries began to spring up within a thirty mile radius of Ernie's. A new degree of respect was now bestowed upon him. Some of his fruit growing neighbors, who used to snicker at his efforts, showed up at his door, hat in hand, asking if he'd be interested in leasing some of their land for grape growing, especially in years when prices for fruit, such as apples, were anemic.

The uniqueness of Ernie's establishment went well beyond the quality of the product. The features of the proprietor made his winery beyond compare. The tasting rooms of other wineries were usually staffed with hired help who were really not involved, rather aloof and who would dispense samples the size of a thimble. Ernie's samples were generous and he usually manned the counter himself and could, and would, tell any potential customer the nature and history of each wine.

Perhaps the best part of the experience at Ernie's tasting room was the relaxed atmosphere. It was his comfortable setting that caused many return visits by customers. When my friends, Dan Frazier and Harold Kinard, would make a trek northward to see me, an afternoon at Ernie's was a given. Not only was the wine good, but also the conversation. With his increased exposure to the public, Ernie became more and more gregarious, although his slow speech remained the same.

Since all of us were involved with a college or university, noble and sometimes great notions on teaching were declared. Often, though, our talk took the form of wraths against administrators, people Ernie labeled as "woodenheads." Ernie felt that by the middle of the eighties, both student and curriculum had been lost on college campuses. In their place the educational institutions had reinserted the morals and workings of capitalism's profits and losses, with accents on management instead of teaching.

Regarding those of us who taught art, Ernie would frequently declare, "You artists prostitute yourselves by teaching." We heartily agreed. This prompted him to create the Artist's Discount whenever he sold us something. When I protested this generosity, his reply was, "This is a family owned business. I'll run it th' hell th' way I want!" I never argued again.

Afternoon discussions and debates weren't limited to just friends. Often customers would suddenly find themselves involved as well in spontaneous parties. None of these events ever got out of hand. Those of a more free-minded persuasion would simply feel compelled to join right in while listening to one of Ernie's many one lined moments of dry humor.

Laughter wasn't always on the menu at Ernie's, though. During periods of what he perceived as a national crisis, customers might be lectured on social values, work ethics, or corruption in government. They might also be the recipients of a finger-wagging sermon on economic injustices such as Reaganomics.

I have never found a wine tasting room like Ernie's. He loomed large, proudly, behind the counter, often wearing a straw hat. At one point he had installed a device he called the Reagan Debtmeter. A device which whirled numbers around and around, day and night, generating a dizzying spiral of increasing value. On several occasions people would get upset with Ernie, such as when some staunch Republicans walked in and spotted the Reagan Debtmeter, then turn around in a huff, without purchasing anything. To which Ernie responded, "I don't give a damn! People who think like that don't deserve my wine."

Ernie's tasting room also possessed a visual charm. Other wineries in the area might finish off their tasting rooms in rough sawn wood, or flashy paneling, posting various images of fancy French vineyards on the walls. At Ernie's, the cinderblock walls were generously covered with photos of family and friends, or of art work given to him by those of us who were beneficiaries of the Artist's Discount. Several of the wall pieces were also given to him by Sid Chafetz, a nationally recognized political and academic satirist. In Sid, Ernie found someone who could pictorially articulate his views of some of the empty pomposity he saw on college campuses, or in congress. Also, on one of the walls, there was a liberal sprinkling of hand lettered quotations from various famous authors and thinkers. Of course, there was also the magnificent view out the large window of the rolling landscape. In other words, when at Ernie's tasting room, one didn't have to stare self-consciously at one's feet while tasting wine. There existed the opportunity to reflect on profound ideas, one's own life, or the universe itself. The room became an extension of Ernie's spirit.

Though I have been gone from the Chippewa Harbor area for some time now, the memory of the wonderful afternoons and the warm comradeship between Ernie and me, as well as with the many friends that I took there to meet him are still fresh and strong. I used to cherish the unexpected phone call, when after a string of gloomy days in the winter, Ernie might call, while sampling a new batch of wine, and declare, "Jaaaack, what this country needs is a damn good housecleaning."

I have the ultimate respect for Ernie. He has been able to mold and create his own outlook on life. He is truly a healthy mix of his broad education in the humanities and the basic values of his humble rural youth. I sometimes catch myself thinking about his oft-repeated phrase, "It's easy to be a simpleton, but hard to be simple."

CHAPTER SEVEN
HOSPITALITY AND
CREATIVITY

With Ernie Bickel's lecture on marital bliss still tumbling around inside of me, my wife Liz and I made a full fledged effort to firmly anchor ourselves to the northern Michigan area. This was most notably done following our first year of marriage. Our first year was spent living in a cramped and crowded apartment, then briefly at a wonderful lake shore cottage before the owner moved back to live there with his new bride. Shortly before we left this lake side cottage it was decided that we would try to purchase our first home. After some looking and help from our friends we found a house just a little way outside of town in North Bay Township. I quickly realized that the results of choosing a place to live and committing to it are the foundations for developing a sense of place and community. I also discovered the importance of neighbors.

Our new house began an exciting and fresh adventure for us. This home quickly became a center for a life that would bring us both great satisfaction for a little more than two decades. The house itself was a graciously anchored, two-story 1880's farmhouse surrounded by three majestic black walnuts, a small grove of evergreens, cedars and even some apple and cherry trees. There were plots of grapevines and ample space for placing flower and vegetable gardens. The house was broad and sturdy and included an additional single story wing for our dining room and kitchen. It had been constructed from locally cut lumber. Beyond the yard were acres of cherry trees; beyond the cherry trees was a view of North Bay and in between; wonderful, rolling hills. As my wife and I stood in the space of our new yard the first day, looking out across the landscape, we felt truly elated and looked forward to starting this phase of our new life together.

After moving in with the assistance of our many friends, we began to discover historical details about the house. These ranged from who the previous owners were, to township hearsay and tidbits about the premises. In fact, one of the township's grand story tellers, Uncle Ferd, lived nearby. Ferd stopped by early on and warned me that in his recollection the foundation and sills for the dining room and kitchen wing hadn't been especially well done. I wanted to verify this bit of hearsay so I went squirming underneath the house to take a look. I did, in fact, notice that one corner was resting on an old cistern and the other corner on a large field stone with nothing in between but the development of a sagging floor. I decided that I would need to shore up some of the addition and with the help of Harold Kinard, did manage to balance out the wing's support system with new lumber and braces. Whether through acts of maintenance, or while entertaining groups of people, this house made us feel at home during our entire time in Chippewa Harbor.

One of the first moments of amazement came right outside our back door during the first spring. We found acres and acres of fruit tree blossoms. The abundant blossoms, although spectacular during daylight, became utterly sublime during the night, under a full moon. To stand amongst the bright blossoms which went out in all directions, twinkling and merging sky with land, was as if taking flight through outer space.

As we began to dig gardens and generally renew our place we quickly discovered the amiable and courteous neighbors. The assortment of people around us opened up a whole new understanding of human nature to me. Not only were these people friendly, but they were generous, honest and remarkably skilled at a variety of tasks.

This sense of neighborliness was genuine and widespread. It was years before these good feelings began to wane and they didn't start until a young farmer named Tom Woodley began to grow beyond his means. Tom probably operated the largest fruit operation in the township when we first moved to the area and was actually quite nice when I first met him. He frequently offered to spray and help with the few fruit trees on our land. However, his desire to expand his business resulted in a false sense of importance and prestige in his mind. This feeling of self-importance and greed was only made worse when he was named to the Board of Directors at the local bank. Chances are they simply felt the need to include a farmer on the board. Unfortunately, this new position went to Tom's head and he began to purchase and expand his operation in questionable, foolish and haphazard ways. Purchasing large quantities of poor land finally took its toll; his fruit sales weren't able to match his expenses. He tried to subdivide and resell portions of his land to quickly cure his miscalculations, but the township refused his requests to do so.

Tom made his last and fatal error when he sold the largest portion of his land to Detroit developers. Soon all of his land was gone and where once stood regional and beautiful orchards quickly remained nothing but the tracks of bulldozers, busily transforming decades of natural progression into a flat and barren landscape. Then, as we all feared, the land was subdivided and replaced with hastily constructed condos and town houses. Overnight Tom went from being a rising star in the township to a widely despised villain. As far as I know he was the first person to sell out to big city developers and, in all of our minds, became somewhat responsible for the slow and steady erosion of the old way of life in the area. To this day the mention of Tom's name brings nothing but looks of scorn and disdain.

Fortunately, prior to the eventual selling off of large portions of local land, I was able to understand and appreciate the old, authentic ways of life. Right across the street from us lived a small fruit farmer named Andy Rogers.

Years before our arrival, Andy and his wife Myrtle had moved back to her father's orchard to fulfill their rural dreams. For a period of time Andy and his wife were able to make a meager but satisfying livelihood off the orchard alone, but over time the market changed and Andy began to take on various odd jobs to supplement their income. Andy could never have been called anything but a hard worker. In addition to his many odd jobs and the orchard, he worked an extremely large vegetable garden which provided his family with food through the summer and on into winter. At the same time Andy would never pass up the chance to engage in friendly conversation. I often spotted him across the road and enjoyed strolling over and conversing on the victories, the woes and various challenges of the world.

Andy possessed the old fashioned Midwestern habits of neighborly etiquette. He was never too busy to help a neighbor. If my car was stuck in one of the frequent snows, sometimes even before I had figured out what to do, Andy would come chugging over in his tractor to pull me out. These sorts of deeds were always done with ease and pleasure. In return I did the same when I could. One time when Andy needed help getting in his cherry crop, I gathered together my friend Freddie Bates and we eagerly helped him bring in the crop. At the end of the day, as was customary for a day of assistance, we sat down to a generous meal at his house.

A few years ago Andy passed away and in addition to losing a friend, yet another symbol of genuine and authentic rural America vanished as well.

Other neighbors of ours, just north about a hundred yards, were the Novotnys. This family was a large collection of jovial and energetic people. They were a classic example of what it meant to be neighbors. They came by shortly after we arrived, as good neighbors do, and introduced themselves to us making us feel quite welcome. For the next twenty years we shared our lives with this family in a close and confident manner. Helping each other without question whenever either of us needed it, lending tools, food, or even running errands. We each offered our time to one another with ease. It was not uncommon for either of us to end up eating dinner at the other's house following an afternoon of help.

Their instant generosity and hospitality were unmatched. They were able to befriend even the occasional visitor. My wife's parents and my own mother visited us from time to time and quickly became fond of the Novotnys. Sometimes, I thought, as anxious to see the Novotnys as they were us.

Contrary to my early childhood opinions of rural citizens, the Novotnys had a creative and eager appetite for life that spread through the whole family. After all, when I was growing up I was led to believe that all farm families were straight arrows, honest, and hard-working, but also sober and conservative people.

The Novotnys lived life to the rumble of a different drummer. Although they may not have set out to be anti-establishment, their creative energy made them so. They were always involved, each of the family members, in some sort of unique project. I often remember Mrs. Novotny busily concocting a recipe for a local or national cooking contest.

The attitudes of the elder Novotnys spread to their two youngest children who stayed on the farm after high school. These two kids were wizards as far as I was concerned. One time they engaged in a remodeling project for their parent's house, doing electrical and plumbing work as easily as someone else might walk. I often gawked at them in open-mouthed amazement, asking them timidly how they knew about plastering, mortar or miter saws and they would always reply, "Oh, that's easy." Well, to me it wasn't easy. I dreaded electrical and plumbing work and only after years and years did I even reach a basic level of competency in carpentry. Yet, to these two youngest Novotnys, difficult tasks were no more than casual, fun projects and no more complicated than tying one's shoe.

My friends and I often shook our heads in utter disbelief when referring to the two youngest Novotny kids. We reverently called them the "neighbor kids." There were times when they would host gigantic parties when their parents might leave town and these parties were always unique and somewhat bizarre. They weren't drunken brawls, but usually exotic, even at times kinky theme parties of some sort, entailing movies and costumes. In the tradition of their mother's desire to concoct new recipes, these parties often entailed equally exotic and appropriate food items. They hosted a spaghetti western one time as well as an array of other theme parties, such as a Hawaiian cookout and a tribute to the Chinese New Year with food and costumes corresponding to the animal of the year, such as a boar, a rabbit, a dragon, or rooster.

Whatever the theme, their parties and life-style were reliably individualized, laced, in a non-aggressive way with hintings of distaste for the status quo. However, it was only their zest and abilities to conjure up original ideas which made them stand out against the more usual ways of living.

As time went by, the youngest Novotny son became an experimental gardener. One of his grand moments came when he created a unique memorial garden to old bowling balls. In amongst a collection of plants lay broken, tarnished, beat up bowling balls and a few bowling pins. The whole project was no more than five feet by five feet. Yet, for whatever reason, this hilarious garden was quite threatening to the new condominium tenants living to the west on some of Tom Woodley's former acreage.

One night in the winter, we awoke to see a set of footprints leading up to and away from the bowling ball garden. All of the bowling balls had been tossed about and the garden formations destroyed, nothing had been spared. We all suspected that this garden and its tribute to individuality was uncomfortable, even hostile to the new, mostly bland, mercenary people moving to the area.

Another of the young son's experiments was with the small trees on the Novotny's land. This son became infatuated with pruning and shaping the trees into pretzels, as well as a crown of thorns, squares and other geometric shapes. At times Mrs. Novotny seemed challenged between feelings of surprise and mirth. Wondering in all honesty, I believe, what her son was capable of.

Over time I realized that the qualities I discovered in the Novotnys existed in many of the students that attended the college. I always felt that the raw and inherent creative energy that existed during my early teaching days in Chippewa Harbor was stronger than anywhere else I've ever been.

CHAPTER EIGHT
FARMERS OF
INDEPENDENCE

In addition to the neighbors, I also became acquainted with some of the old, third generation farmers in the township. Although others may have found these farmers crusty old men, I found them remarkable. They were fiercely independent men who firmly believed in the right to live as one pleased. Without large bank notes, or the eyes of a large corporation looking over their shoulders, these men assumed it was their duty and right to take care of themselves. I met many of these farmers through my neighbors, but also through some of my students as well as at the annual pancake and fund-raising dinners I liked to attend. When I heard stories about the old farmers in the area at local grocery stores and township meeting halls, I listened with fascination. After all, many of these farmers were as much legend as they were real. Just as I had with the Stanleyville Intellectuals, I curiously admired these old farmer's behaviors and life-styles and when I encountered them, or overheard stories about them, would listen with open and respectful ears.

One of the first farmers I met was Anthony Kratochvil, who was the grandfather of one of my students. My first encounter with Anthony was a result of my interest in doing landscape drawings. His granddaughter, Mary, had overheard me wishing to find a new spot in the countryside to draw during class one day and informed me that her grandfather had a farm I could wander around on. Shortly thereafter, a time was set up for me to come out to the farm. Her grandfather eyed me curiously at first when I arrived, but being a teacher of his granddaughter, he grudgingly accepted me. I was immediately awestruck by the pure beauty of his farm. There was a fine old barn built in the early 1900's, as well as nicely tended and maintained fruit storage and packing sheds. As Mary gave me an initial tour of the landscape, I was witness to wonderful stands of fruit trees, gorgeous valleys and dense old hardwoods. I was left with an open invitation to explore their land. I returned a number of times by myself and got to know Anthony quite well.

It wasn't long before Anthony and I were able to engage in good conversation. He was a rather short, rotund man, with a sad, suntanned face, but he did have a wonderfully dry sense of humor. He was also a generous man, when apples were in season I would more often than not leave with a bagful. This generosity also extended to the old fashioned Damsen plums that he grew. This remarkable fruit was the base for a locally popular, township liquor. I remember well when he gave me enough of these plums to make my own liquor. This elixir involved combining an alcohol base of one's choice, with extra sugar and the plums. The mixture then spent three miraculous months soaking together. Around Thanksgiving time the drinking would begin. We all knew of this concoction as Plum Bounce.

Often times Anthony and I spoke about the college and how it was run and in later years we began to speak about land development. Knowing I was staunchly opposed to development he would often point across one of his beautiful hillsides and comment on what a marvelous golf course his land would make. At which point I would become aggravated and irritated. It was during a moment like this that one could almost make out a smile on Anthony's face. However, this was not to be confused with his real feelings. His independence was firm and fierce. He did not accept outside government, or zoning board decisions in a favorable fashion. Any government ideas which came from outside the local township were viewed as purely invasive.

One time, following a successful drawing session, I saw Anthony refueling his tractor and went over to tell him that an attempt to develop some land by my house had been defeated. I also mentioned that I had spoken with a neighbor of his, Raymond Shaw, and relayed that Raymond was opposed to development as well. Anthony's opinion of Raymond, however, came as a surprise to me. Anthony declared, after a long pause, "Raymond Shaw is a NEWCOMER! He knows nothing about this township." This was the end of the conversation. Anthony stalked off, mounted his tractor and drove away. Well, considering that Ray Shaw had lived in the area over forty years, I instantly felt smaller than ever, especially since I had only been in the area maybe eight years by then.

I continued to explore Anthony's farm after Mary graduated from the college. In fact, after Mary graduated she became quite involved in the Local Arts Council, hosting memorable winter sledding parties which would culminate at her family's big farm house around a large cauldron of chili. Sadly, after Mary was married she slowly lost touch with those of us in the arts.

Another man of shadows and legend was Grover Simpson, a true living myth at the northern end of the township. He was truly as hard to discover as a wolf. One time I did catch a view of him from afar, dressed in a gray shirt and pants with yellow suspenders. On another occasion, I got to stand by him in the township hall during an election. Grover was quite fond of chewing tobacco and while he was waiting in line to vote, he made several trips to the window to expel streams of tobacco juice. These streams went flying downwards, only to land, with a loud snapping noise, on the tops of the cars parked below. His true character could more or less be summed up with this act. He was a man who lived with an honorable, direct and unswerving sense of individuality. Any perceived, negative side effects of this way of life were deemed insignificant by him.

A good example of this sense of individuality occurred when the state health department ordered Grover to upgrade his seasonal worker's housing. Well Grover would have none of this. He was not going to be told by anybody at the state capital what to do. He could manage very well by himself. Then, out of principle I suppose, Grover went to jail in defiance of this order for a brief while, maintaining his honor and proving that he would not cave in to the state telling him what to do.

Yet another notable farming family in the township was the Weaver household. They symbolized the sense of independence in yet another way. This family was well-educated, in fact both Mr. and Mrs. Weaver were well-respected scholars from the big state University down near Detroit. They had, however, owned their farmland many years by the time I arrived. The Weavers ran their farm as a sort of independent republic. They were known far and wide as a place where free spirits, musicians, "hippies," or for that matter, even a Democrat might be welcome to stay, work and feel welcome. I was drawn to this farm for many reasons, not least for the landscape and the drawings it inspired. I always looked forward to ending a day of drawing in their company, discussing timely and scholarly issues. If I was really lucky it would be the cherry harvest and a large bowl of the most beautiful and delicious cherries would be placed in front of me.

A day at the Weaver's refuge/farm was always a valuable experience and just like the other farmers I met, they were determined to live their own lives the way they wanted. Just as one should be allowed to up in the Northwoods, or anywhere in our nation for that matter.

CHAPTER NINE
THE ECCENTRIC APPLE
MERCHANT

One is prone to remembering the old days with an exaggerated and sometimes overly sympathetic tone, as if in some way, back when we were younger and more able to defend ourselves against change things were better, clearer, easier, certainly more fun. I have tried to avoid these sentiments for the most part and will continue to do so. However, I truly believe that the world I enjoyed in northern Michigan changed in an uncontrollable fashion with the increased arrival of short-term, summer tourists. Over time our area seemed to take on the atmosphere of a traveling circus as hordes of dim-witted, fast-moving tourists made haste through town. Most of these fly-by tourists seemed to hold an irritated contempt for the local residents, treating us like flat bread dough. Perhaps they hoped we would beckon to their every call, maybe pose for them as if we were part of a cute post card, expecting us to be backwood yokels, mistreated step children on our knees like Cinderella.

Summer visitors hadn't always been so suspect though. On the other end of this tourist spectrum were the families who had owned vacation property for years, families who were primarily from a rich and genteel tradition. Those, who in earlier days had been able to arrive via train, or even lake steamers. These families used to appear with the greening of the leaves, sometimes bringing along nannies and helpers and extended families to enjoy summers of slow relaxation. The summers for these people were as if extracted from a chapter of *The Great Gatsby* and the colorful, jazzy words of F. Scott Fitzgerald. These traditional, wealthier, summer residents, due to their permanence and commitment to the area, seemed to blend in and support the community rather than exploit it. They were, of course, quite wealthy, yet they seemed, for the most part, to be quiet, as well as respectful of the local residents and our yearlong customs. I always believed that these people appreciated what the area had to offer in terms of solitude and natural beauty. This was in stark opposition to the style of tourist that began to travel through later on with haste and impatience, hoping to be provided with a good time just because they had decided to show up.

A memorable and eccentric member of this class of longtime, summer resident was an old lady named Tessie Garrison. As nearly as I could discover, her family had been landowners since the late 1920's. The land she returned to each summer was quite diverse and lovely. The estate was anchored by a large, old late nineteenth century farm house, with long narrow windows spaced evenly all along the sides. The Garrisons property was about forty acres in size, with twenty battered acres of old apple orchards and a few more acres of beautiful woods which ran down a slope, to a beach on North Bay. Hidden amongst these woods by the lake were three 1920's guest cottages. For a good many years I had no idea that the Garrisons existed. Their land was not in a high traffic area, and certainly the Garrisons themselves, who only consisted of Tessie by this time, were not, and had not been, a boisterous bunch.

My first encounter with Tessie was during an end-of-the-summer party I held for my friends prior to the start of a new academic year. In an effort to say farewell to the summer air and season of good fun, a group of us piled into my friend Dan Frazier's ageing van and headed off to the northern tip of the township where there was an historic lighthouse. We often went to this area to get away, and although the beach front was somewhat rocky, its lonely spirit always proved refreshing. The beach and lighthouse were part of an undeveloped area in the township. The land behind the beach was a rugged, deep green forest which made things feel even more isolated and relaxing. We would all walk along, skipping stones, sometimes jumping in for a swim, listening to the waves break upon the shore.

It was during this trip, on our way back from a long afternoon of mirth, when I encountered a small, dumpy looking lady in the parking lot selling apples to hapless tourists from the back seat of a rusty, Dodge Dart station wagon. This lady was certainly a pathetic site to behold. Her clothing was torn up, thin and faded; she was wearing some mismatched tennis shoes full of holes; and upon her head sat a floppy, windblown straw hat. Curious, I walked over and became somewhat irritated at the essentially rotten quality of the merchandise she was vending. The baskets of apples she was trying to peddle were greenish-yellow and lumpy, completely undeveloped. Not only was her appearance dumpy, but her pleas to potential customers were rather shoddy and pitiful. I recall thinking this old lady looked poverty stricken. If it weren't for my own basket of apples at home, I probably would have bought some from her, out of a sense of pity to help this appalling looking lady in need of a bit of luck.

A few weeks later, when visiting with my friends, the Weavers, I discovered who this apple lady was. The Weavers knew much about the area, especially about the various longtime summer residents. They themselves being a well established family from Detroit who had bought up some of the orchard land in the township.

While I was recounting the sight of this old and tattered lady to the Weavers, I was quickly interrupted, "Oh Good Grief! That must have been Tessie." Upon further explanation I came to understand that not only wasn't Tessie the least bit poor, but rather, she may have been one of the wealthiest individuals in the township.

It turned out that the saga of Tessie was quite unique. Tessie was the quirky daughter of the Garrison family. The family had owned the land in northern Michigan for some seventy years now, but in recent years only Tessie continued to visit. I quickly realized, however, as is often the case with eccentrics, that what was really known about the ways of Tessie were small scattered bits of truth, alongside hefty smatterings of exaggeration and hearsay. Since Tessie and the Garrison family had never been very social members of the community, merely summer residents, what was really known might better be considered legend.

It turned out that the Garrisons had accumulated wealth down in central Michigan from a wholesale bakery supply company. Tessie was the only remaining Garrison, the Weavers had decided. At least the only Garrison who still had any desire to return to the land in northern Michigan. Everyone knew when she was staying at the old house too, for she would hang the United States flag, as well as the United Nations flag from her front porch flag poles. People claimed that she was a United Nation's groupie. In fact, I was told that after years and years of presenting petitions and social causes to the U.N.'s General Assembly in New York, she had finally been kicked out permanently from even entering the U.N. building.

All the information about Tessie, who could actually have purchased half the township, caught my curiosity. So that the next time Dan Frazier came to town, the two of us took off down the beach to have a look around the Garrison estate. I felt I must know more. When we got to the beach front property of the Garrisons, we looked around and cautiously entered the woods.

At first we quietly worked our way to the three guest cottages and peeked inside. They had been neglected for years and were showing early signs of dilapidation. Neither of us could imagine when the last person had been there. Each cabin was well built, however, and through the dust and grime, one could sense that the cabins had once been very tastefully designed, wood and log buildings.

When we peered into the sun porch of one of the cabins, we saw a table set for four. Apparently a dinner had been planned, but never served, many years ago. A scene from Miss Havaslam's dining room in *Great Expectations* flashed through my mind.

Ed Weaver seemed to remember an incident that might have explained this. Years ago he remembered a yacht sailing into the bay and two individuals rowing into the shore near the cabins. He watched these two individuals walk up and inspect one of the cabins for a few minutes, but then the two had turned around and returned to their yacht, pulled anchor and sailed away, never to be seen again.

After Dan and I examined the cottages, we stole up the path to the big house through the old orchard. We moved cautiously, so as not to be seen. Although there was no one there to see us, we still felt compelled to move sheepishly and silently.

On the east end of the orchard was a grove of large maple trees. Then underneath these trees we found a curious wonderland. There was a wooden replica of a Greco-Roman balustrade and in front, an old, weed-choked reflecting pool. As we examined these things, we felt a large amount of respect for the old, and now suffering, family estate. We sensed the dreams and eccentric spirit of Tessie and her family around us.

When we returned, and I told the Weavers what we had found, they told me that when Tessie was younger she had become rather attached to the movie, *Three Coins in the Fountain*, which included a large marble balustrade and reflecting pool. She had compulsively requested replicas be made and then hauled to the estate, beneath the maples. As I was told this I sat spellbound at the clever and isolated fantasy world she had designed for herself on this land. I felt I may have shared some of her attachment to the land and why, even as such an old lady, she continued to return each year. She was able to live her life of fantasy, fulfilling what she believed, or wanted her life to be along the shore of North Bay. I considered, given the opportunity, who wouldn't want to live a make-believe life on their own private woods? I was taken away with the idea myself.

Some of the public legend regarding Tessie was her terrible driving habits. She was often seen driving along the curvy road by the lake intensely reading a magazine, or newspaper. Even a good driver needed to pay attention to the road from Tessie's estate to town, but not Tessie, she let poor driving get the upper hand. On one occasion, many years before my arrival, she was said to be driving her mother into town when she missed a curve, sending the two of them off the road, into North Bay, knee deep in water. At this point, Tessie told her mother to wait and that she would go for help. Well, unfortunately, while walking in to fetch assistance Tessie became sidetracked and it wasn't until many hours later that she remembered her mother, who was still sitting knee deep in water, inside the car, in the lake. Remembering her mission, Tessie arranged for help, returned, retrieving both car and mother.

Calling Tessie a cheapskate would be an understatement. Rumor had it that Tessie wanted to maintain the quality of the family orchard, but at the same time was unwilling to pay much, if anything, to do so. As fate would have it, because an unsprayed orchard in the neighborhood could cause great distress to others, Tessie's orchard was often sprayed and tended to by others at no expense, just to keep it from becoming a cesspool of fungus, pests and other problems which might have easily damaged other's efforts at trying to make a living by apple growing.

In addition, Tessie would never allow "professional," seasonal apple pickers to harvest her apples. This was far too large an expense in her mind. Instead, she would call upon the helpless and innocent young children in the area to help her out. In reality Tessie more or less tricked the kids into helping. Rarely did she actually pay anything for their services. Instead, she would come up with what she thought to be a reasonable payment, such as taking the children to an outdoor music concert for a few hours in exchange for several days spent in the hot sun, picking apples for her.

Once she had finished tricking kids into picking and gathering her apples, she would place the fruit in wooden cherry lugs and drive her apples down to the processing plant. It was quite a sight really, this rich old lady, in her beat up station wagon, taking a place in line with the massive, industrial sized fruit trucks, waiting to be paid for her overripe and lumpy fruit. The processing people, to avoid any trouble and to cease the exaggerated beggary and pleas that Tessie would utter if her apples were not accepted, would go ahead and pay her a few dollars just to get her out of their hair.

What always amazed me, and somewhat bothered me, was the extreme measures that this rich lady would go to save a few pennies. Perhaps this is how the rich become rich: hoarding their money and sharing their wealth with no one. It was a stark contrast really—she possessed so much wealth, yet rarely paid anyone for anything. She presented herself in such pathetic fashion that people ended up helping her not so much to be nice, but because they felt sorry and pity for her.

It was in the late eighties that Tessie finally stopped arriving during the summer. The Weavers noticed that the land was finally put up for sale one summer and no one has ever seen Tessie again. It was assumed, by all of us, that she had passed away, putting an end to the Garrisons as summer residents in the area.

The disappearance of Tessie also seemed to mark the loss of a certain life-style up north. One rarely encounters the old time, genteel, summer resident— entertaining visitors and family members in lake front cottages, summer after summer. Not to mention entertaining their fantasy wonderland imaginations summer after summer in a reflecting pool beneath large and aging trees.

CHAPTER TEN
THE HIGH PRIEST
OF BEDLAM

Normally I was not in trouble with the staff at Sladek's. In fact, I was rather well behaved over the years except for joining in during instances of occasional loud cheer. Many, such as the public school teachers, or the group of state hospital workers, whom I called the Mod Squad, would gather during Friday evenings to let off the steam of a full week of work. I often felt a bit troubled with the loud evenings when they occurred. I was always torn because I couldn't deny that I enjoyed the noisy revelry, yet I also missed the quiet atmosphere from when old Henry Sladek kept things hushed and a person was better able to carry on engaging, relaxing conversation.

There was one day, however, when things seriously altered my usual pattern at Sladek's. This happened when I was put in charge of entertaining a visiting artist that had been recommended by a friend of mine to exhibit his work at the college. This artist proved to be a one-man wrecking crew. The afternoon and evening and all the moments in between still stand out as being both hilarious and embarrassing for me. I managed to get kicked out of Sladek's not just once, but twice during it all.

The visiting artist was Seamus O'Malley, a photographer who had recently been hired to work at Lake Huron University. He had quite a history surrounding him. I was to learn that most of his background was not conducive to a gentle evening of sipping cocktails, discussing art theory and reflecting on art technique. Rather, he was a neurotic, pompous, irritating and egotistical man, not to mention, on heavy doses of strong back pain medication which didn't mix well with booze. I had been told, prior to meeting him, that he had been released from the Army due to some sort of nervous condition. I found out this was not an exaggeration. He was a madman and a maniac, a complete and utter wacko! I also learned, that prior to his artist career he had traveled across the country dressed as a Catholic priest. Forging together a phony credit card, he had spent a summer traveling in slathering luxury at expensive hotels, exotic restaurants and hip lounges. When confronted by some suspicious employee about his identity, he would simply make a phone call to a New York Bishop, a friend of his, an impersonator as well, who would assure anyone asking that Seamus had approval from the Diocese to use the credit card. As Seamus had stringy, shoulder length hair, a poorly trimmed beard and snaggly teeth, it must have been a real sight to observe him in his Priest robe, coaxing free hotel rooms with his phony credit card.

Seamus arrived in town with Floyd Hempstead, another member of the Lake Huron University art staff. Floyd was a burly and hostile individual, as well as being extremely overweight. A first glance at his unruly beard and chubby face reminded one of a portly, unkempt and shaggy maned warthog. He had also, many years ago, taken on the role of perpetual drunk. Floyd, Seamus and I hung Seamus' photos for the exhibition, and I shortly discovered that this would be the only period of time with any rationality.

We then cantered off to Sladek's for lunch and beers. It wasn't long after we finished eating that Seamus became loud and obnoxious. Everyone in the tavern became quite annoyed with Seamus' hysterical laughter. We finally got kicked out after Seamus started singing with operatic gusto about a dairy cow, "Missus O'Leary's caooow kicked over the lahntern and burnt Chicaaaago dooowne. Thestoopidsonofabitch!!!" For some reason this song was utterly hilarious to Seamus and he cranked his level of laughter up another notch as we were all sent through the front door.

Standing outside, I noticed that my friend Freddie Bates had joined the group. Since it was well before time to attend the evening's activities at the college, we went off to the Oaken Bucket, another bar in town, where once again Seamus and Floyd became loud and incorrigible. When a customer complained about our behavior, Floyd told him, in a staccato manner, "If ya don't like it Buddy, there's the door!" At this point, all the customers, including the bartender, became irate at these two strangers. Floyd, a rather ugly drunk, probably realized that telling a regular customer to leave was not going to work. We were soon asked to depart, which we did, but only under the threat of the police being called.

Outside the Oaken Bucket, confronted with a parking lot and the blaringly bright sun, our group of misfits stood dazed and lost. There were two car loads of us. Knowing we had to go someplace, Seamus joined Freddie Bates in one car and I jumped in the car with Floyd and his tawdry girlfriend. Then, for some reason we went toward my house, probably because my wife was in bed with bronchitis and I needed to check on her. On the way to my house a race soon developed between the two drivers which carried us at high speeds over the grounds of the high school, across several lawns in a sedate and well manicured subdivision of town and through a portion of the city golf course. Upon approaching my house in the country, I impulsively yelled, "Floyd, let's race 'em through the orchard!" So we did. We careened down the lane toward Ghering's old orchard, with Seamus and Freddie in hot pursuit. Several sliding turns were performed on the long, wet grass. Floyd ran down a dead, brittle tree and put yet another dent in his battered station wagon. The bone dry wood had exploded into a thousand pieces that flew through the air like shrapnel. On the way back to my house Seamus and Freddie cheated and drove across my lawn to win the race amidst howls of insane glee. All of us were screaming and laughing like a pack of crazy banshees.

Floyd and I cautiously entered the house to see how Liz was doing. Upon entering the bedroom, it was quite obvious to me that she was all right, but that the sight of us was disgusting to her. Floyd, for all his previous bravado, sheepishly announced that we should leave now and go to the Humanities Division fall party and Seamus' opening. I could hear Seamus bellowing outside. Looking at my wife for a brief moment I understood the shameful and outrageous manner in which we had all been behaving, but these feelings only lasted a moment. Off we went, snorting with laughter, to the college.

Since I was part of the Humanities Division I was expected to be in attendance. In addition, I was responsible for delivering Seamus, the party's guest of honor, but who I now knew was a complete maniac and far too drunk to be coherent. It would have helped out everyone if I hadn't delivered Seamus, but at the time I was determined to follow orders, plus, there would be food at the party and we were all in need of nourishment.

As I had thought, it would have been better not to have taken Seamus to his opening and faculty party. He was abominable and crass to everyone. There was no female in attendance who wasn't embarrassed and outraged by his remarks. No student whose questions weren't made fun of, no faculty member's hand shaken that Seamus didn't offend. When asked what he thought about art, he blurted out, in drunken slobbery, "IT'S ALL ART. ALL ART, GOD ... DAMN ... IT!" When asked his opinion on art critics, he loudly proclaimed, "THEY SHOULD ALL BE GASSED, THE BASTARDS. ALL BE GASSED. ALL OF THEM."

For a brief moment during the gathering Seamus did settle down, but his silence was merely a result of his searching the cabinets of the room for additional booze. During his silence Seamus did manage to find the department's reserved supply of liquor. Then, while sitting there drinking from a bottle of rye whiskey, Floyd snuck up behind him and said, "Hey Seamus, you're awfully quiet. You some kind of sissy, or sump'n?" That was all it took. This comment unleashed another volley of shouting and hyena-like laughter which was even more crude and mean spirited than before.

As Seamus continued to shout irrational comments I finally had to take him away with Freddie. In the meantime, much to my displeasure, after getting Seamus all riled up again, Floyd had high tailed it out of town and returned to Lake Huron University with his girlfriend, leaving Seamus behind. Not knowing where to go, I returned with the screaming and psychotic Seamus to Sladek's. It wasn't long before Seamus was spilling beer and slurring out offensive comments. Once again, he and I and Freddie were kicked out. This was the first and only time in my life that I have been asked to leave two bars, three times, in one day.

Fortunately, Freddie begrudgingly agreed to take Seamus home that night. I certainly wouldn't have been able to take him to my house for the evening, as Liz wouldn't have tolerated his out-of-control presence. As I returned home I understood that the day had been a wreck. Freddie told me that the next morning Seamus actually acted subdued and sheepish, probably because of a lack of rejuvenated brain particles.

In my later years I wondered if I ought to be ashamed of this series of events, yet I can't help but look back at the day of dionysian episodes with a certain wry smile. The day's mirth and madness is certainly something that few people experience. I can still recall people staring out their windows as we raced by in our cars yelling at the top of our lungs. Our trail that day left people horror stricken and open-mouthed all across town. I am always able to think back on the insanity of Seamus and bring forth a good hearty chuckle.

CHAPTER ELEVEN
"NOT TO WORRY"

A nother dedicated migrant to town and someone who deserves his own chapter was my friend Herb Loftus. Herb arrived in Chippewa Harbor disenchanted with big city life; yearning for a simpler, more basic life-style in a small town. As a sculptor, he had decided he would continue creating art, yet be able to market his work in the city, exploiting what he considered the advantages of living in a small town, but having connections in a large urban area. His intentions were noble. However, his plans didn't often go the way he had hoped.

I first met Herb at a meeting of the local arts council and discovered that he had studied at the Crandale Art Academy, a rather prestigious art school in the Detroit area, and was a veteran of the navy. His wife, it turned out, had relatives in the area.

I often met interesting people at the local arts council in the early seventies. This art group was remarkably lively and seemed to attract many of the migrating professionals in town. These people were genuinely aware of culture and wanted to support and integrate the arts into the life and ways of the town. It wasn't until the mid-eighties that any of us began to notice a lack of this cultural spirit in new members and new residents. These later migrants, "yuppies," seemed distant, boring and in attendance more to be seen, than heard. The money these people seemed willing to spend for fancy cars and houses rarely left their pocketbooks in support of the local arts council, or the art work of local residents.

It didn't take me long to become Herb's friend. His easy going attitude and pleasant, offbeat sense of humor, as well as his festive drinking habits, made him quite fun to be with. He soon became known by everyone in the local art scene as a voracious volunteer and willing exhibitor, not to mention, a lively spirit.

What set Herb apart from many other artists in the area was his strong affinity for various and sundry, distilled and fermented products. He could always be counted upon to join in with any revelry or celebration. Such was the case when my dear Uncle Louie passed away in Croatia. Following this news I immediately sought out Herb for comfort, and together we hoisted many glasses of spirits in honor of my departed Uncle and comrade. It was this sort of willingness to be with people that endeared me to Herb. I can think of no time when Herb wasn't in good spirits. He was always ready to pay homage to any celebration, whether it was a deceased relative, a funeral, a birthday, or just Bulgarian National Week.

When Herb and his wife moved to town they purchased an older home in the heart of the downtown area. He quickly restored and enlarged the garage into an adequate studio for himself. However, almost every project after the garage studio, such as moving walls and tiling floors inside the house, were rarely completed. It was clear, as I got to know Herb, that he didn't take life too seriously. Many people soon began to consider him more of a wastrel, or no-account, than an artist. However, I rather admired Herb's calmness. I found him a welcome and refreshing relief. It is tiresome the way many of us take life so seriously, becoming intensely involved with projects, brooding over mistakes and poor judgments. Herb didn't suffer from this sort of behavior. He never broke into angry spells, nor did he seem to feel disappointment, or the frustrations many of us do when making a mistake. Rather than the usual stream of curses associated with error or mishap, Herb would simply shrug his shoulders, utter a rapid-fire giggle and start over again.

I often met Herb prior to attending one of the many fund-raising events for the local Art's Council. It was not out of the question that prior to going to a fundraiser we would partake of a few preliminary drinks. Our various and energetic salutes, prior to the events, often caused us to develop a healthy glow, and on a few occasions made us, in particular Herb, quite a sight on the dance floor. He would often appear limp and loose like a rag doll, emitting laughter and a devil-may-care smile. He was never hostile or belligerent though. Herb was deftly skilled at riding the goofy footed waves of feeling good.

Herb's happy-go-lucky attitude toward life had a way of spilling over into his art work. It wasn't that his work was of poor quality, or even poorly done. In fact, he was a fine craftsman with clever and creative ideas. Unfortunately he was rarely able to accomplish anything in a reasonable amount of time. When he got a commission, for instance, things didn't usually proceed as the customer might hope or reasonably expect. When questioned or reminded of what needed to be done he would simply shrug his shoulders, snicker and flip his arms to the side.

"Not to worry," he'd repeat over and over, "not to worry."

A perfect example of this occurred when a new Catholic Church was being built in town and many of the local artists were commissioned to do work. I had always touted this as a great idea since there was plenty of talent in town, including the skills of Herb. Herb once again became a challenge though. For the most part, all of the artists involved had completed their work two to three weeks ahead of time so that on the dedication day, everything would be in place. Herb, on the other hand, was nowhere to be seen, in fact many of us doubted if he had even started his project. Everyone involved sat on pins and needles, wondering what would happen.

Herb had been assigned to do some bronze plaques to depict and commemorate various biblical scenes for the front doors, as were sometimes seen on older Italian Renaissance cathedrals. Just as many of us suspected, it wasn't until a week prior to the dedication that Herb arranged to cast these bronze plaques at the college foundry.

On the day of the casting, the furnace was fired up and roaring. A few assistants were on hand to offer help. Legend has it that Herb arrived a tad late and may have been a bit under the influence of some sort of distilled beverage. Anyway, the rich, molten metal was poured into the molds which shortly thereafter blew up. Then, as was his way, Herb merely shrugged his shoulders and calmly stated that he'd have to start over again. Much to everyone's surprise, Herb did get back to work and the plaques were finished and installed at the church one day before the public dedication ceremony. During the dedication ceremony, I looked over at Herb who was broadly grinning and enjoying the ceremony. The words, "Not to worry, not to worry," started running through my mind. Why had any of us ever questioned him?

Herb's carefree life-style was wide reaching. Shortly after arriving in town he developed the desire to be a sailor. He latched on to a boat and although he did become a rather decent sailor, his navigation skills were close to deplorable. He was frequently lost and being rescued by the Coast Guard, who would have to go out and guide him into shore. None of this was aided by his desire to drink vodka while pretending to be a sea captain.

As if a Roman candle, Herb continued to drink and celebrate life at a heightened pitch. One year at his in-law's Fourth of July party at an orchard in the country, Herb, already quite giddy from an overindulgence of mai tai's and red wine, worked his way on top of a chicken coop. Once atop the coop he declared, to the gathering of curious people, "Watch closely, I'm going to fly." Of course, Herb landed flat on his face in the tall grass. He lay on the ground without moving, maybe five to ten seconds, slowly raised his head, one of his front teeth chipped, before he broke into a wail of laughter. "What a flight!" he declared.

About a year after the completion of his work for the church, Herb began to pursue the idea of "getting back to the land." Herb explored this desire to be with the land the hard way. The day he decided he needed to begin working with the land, he signed on with an apple picking crew for the fall. It wasn't long after spending hours in the sun that Herb's idea of being with the land began to fade. It shortly became clear that crew work was not a joy ride. The need to get the fruit off the trees was demanding and timely. Herb's desire to work the land for a living didn't last through the season.

Another activity that Herb deemed essential to a man living in harmony with the land was to heat one's home with a wood stove. Of course, as was his way, Herb came up with this opinion on the coldest day of the winter. Determined to implement his new idea immediately, Herb turned off his furnace, got out his chisel and hammer and began to bang out a hole in his chimney to attach the flue for his new wood stove. As the cold air began to rush in around his poorly chiseled hole, Herb sat down and clutched his head. He was suffering from a tremendous hangover. I happened to walk in during the beginning of this project and got to listen to Herb yell out each time he whacked the chisel into the bricks. His head must have been ringing like the bells of Notre Dame. I could barely believe my eyes and ears as this project unfolded. I offered to help, but

Herb would have none of it. "Everything is under control," he assured me, "everything is fine."

Once this wood stove was finally installed the second part of the chore involved a nearly constant feeding of wood. Having become a part-time employee of the college, Herb had noticed a dead tree alongside one of the busier streets through campus. As a result of his good charm, Herb was granted permission to cut this tree down for fuel. All was fine until Herb miscalculated the felling of the tree and it plopped across the street while everyone was on their way home from work. With the tree across the road, chaos occurred for the hour or so in which it took Herb to finally cut up and clear the wood from the street. Amidst the sound of honking car horns and his sputtering chain saw, one could hear the light hearted giggle of Herb while he worked on trimming and cutting the wood, occasionally waving to the upset drivers, assuring them everything was under control.

Herb explained to me one afternoon that once a person commits himself to the alternative life-style of the wood stove, he needs one additional item to become truly competent: a hefty pickup truck. For one thing, a truck would carry more wood than the family sedan. A truck, declared Herb, would complete his quest to become an adept woodsman. So off Herb went, in search of the ideal vehicle to compliment both his wood stove and newly discovered woodsman's image.

One winter evening, Herb was searching through the classified section of the newspaper when he found an affordable pickup truck for sale. The next day, he drove through the snow covered alley behind the address listed in the advertisement, in search of this truck, but he couldn't find it.

Herb pulled out into the street and parked in front of the residence. He walked up the front steps and rang the bell. When a man answered the door, Herb asked about the truck for sale. The owner asked, "Didn't you see it out back?"

Herb answered, "Well ... no. Just a lot of snow back there." The man led Herb through the house, to the back porch where he grabbed a broom. "C'mon, I'll show ya."

The two of them walked out the back door and approached a pile of snow. The man began sweeping and soon a window emerged, then a rusty door, then a sun-faded hood and dented fender. The owner opened the door and handed Herb the keys. "Start 'er up," he said. Herb slid on to the tattered seat, inserted the key and the engine roared into action.

That evening, I received an excited phone call from Herb. "Jack, I found a truck! The license plate even has my initials and birthday numbers on it. I gotta have it! I just gotta!"

I remember a letter I had written to one of my friends explaining Herb's new truck:

"Herb has just bought a pickup truck. An old battered heap, doors falling off, rusty, windows broken, but with the license plates matching his initials and birthday so he just had to have it. He tried fixing the heater but was driving along when the heater started blowing out steam. The steam froze on the windshield and soon he couldn't see out. I don't know how Herb has survived so long, I just don't know. He was out to my house today cutting firewood with a chain saw and there was wood falling all over him. Herb just doesn't take life very seriously."

What I forgot to mention in this early letter was that after the windows froze over on the truck, Herb continued to drive. Soon he was off the road, narrowly missing a grove of big cedar trees. Once he came to a stop, he only slightly admitted defeat by opening his window and driving back on to the road and down the street with his head sticking out the open window.

Time and patience began to take a toll on Herb. His free wheeling life-style could not last forever. His drinking habits alone were destined to lead him to hard times. After a few years in town, Herb's wife could take it no longer. She just couldn't handle what she and society considered his irresponsible behavior.

Herb was cast out of his home in the dead of winter. With no money, he only had one place to go, his sailboat. Of course, his sailboat was frozen solid in the ice, but it was better than living under a bridge. He packed a few clothes and some possessions to begin what must have been an extremely unhappy and lonely winter. He was lonely for many reasons, but primarily since he was faced with the outlook of changing the course of his life. Most of his friends and family had lost their patience with his antics of the past few years.

I visited him a few times during the winter and his boat was surprisingly warm and comfortable. One time, during a mighty blizzard, his hatch cover blew off, though. Then, as the cover went blowing down the beach like a tumbleweed, out went Herb as well, dashing after the hatch cover, in his stocking feet, through piles and drifts of snow. It was truly a gloomy and destitute sight to behold this grown man so down on his luck. Although, when I retold the story at Sladek's, it provoked a hearty round of laughter from everyone, myself included.

There was another sad portion of Herb's winter in the sailboat which brought about hoots and howls back on the mainland in Sladek's. One evening Herb was drinking with another destitute individual, also harbored up in a sailboat for the winter. The two men had developed a friendship and began drinking together. Then, as isolation and poverty are prone to doing, the art of concoction began to play a valuable part in the two men's drinking habits. On this particular night, when the other man was visiting Herb's boat, they were enjoying a specially prepared elixir of vodka and powdered orange juice. Herb proudly referred to this new invention as the poor man's screwdriver.

During this particular evening things became pretty heated. The other man, it turned out, had a wooden leg and while the two of them were engaged in drinking, the other man must have placed his wooden leg too close to Herb's stove, because his wooden leg began to smolder and catch on fire. Needless to say, this story was met with an appropriate mixture of pity, amazement and laughter.

Finally, as the winter ended, Herb placed his boat on a trailer and left town to find another style of life. He returned to town a couple of years later, with a new wife and, to everyone's amazement, no liquor aboard.

I haven't seen Herb in years now, but I know that when I do see him again we will pick up where we left off: with good cheer, laughter and a warm sense of friendship. Just the way it should be.

Chapter Twelve
The Dumb Farmer

During the twenty years I spent in the Chippewa Harbor area, one of the most interesting characters was Luther Runquist. I met Luther during my first year at Tamarack College. He was a member of the Board of Trustees and would often make unannounced and informal appearances around campus in order to examine, first hand, how the college was operating. He enjoyed observing those who were in the teaching trenches, so to speak, and wanted to learn how the whole institution worked from the grass roots up, rather than from a flashy, four color brochure, or over conversation during an expensive dinner.

My first encounter with Luther was between classes right outside the Fine Arts Building one autumn afternoon, during the zenith of fall colors. I was introduced to him by Warren Baker, the director of the Humanities Division. While standing beside Warren, I noticed, ambling up the walk from afar, an intriguing-looking, stocky man with a square Scandinavian face. As this man drew nearer I saw that he was dressed in an aging brown suit and a reddish tie that had seen better days. My boss waved his arm and as he did, the stocky man broke into a genuinely warm smile. They joked between themselves and then I was introduced. Warren introduced him as, "Luther Runquist, the only honest man on the Board of Trustees."

Luther responded with an observation on the school's new Fine Arts Building, "Warren, this fine building of yours, with its high ceilings would sure make a good place to store hay."

Then, after a bit more bantering between the two, Luther looked at me and said, "Don't pay any attention to what I say. I'm just a dumb farmer."

Well, as I began to know Luther better, I quickly discovered that he was dumb like a fox. He possessed a keen awareness of common sense and was able to censor that which was mere frivolity. He was known to bring a board meeting back to earth with some simple but logical observation.

With each successive appearance Luther made, either in the faculty lunchroom or in our building, I continued to learn more of his story. He was born on a farm about twenty-five miles southeast of Chippewa Harbor in an area called Drum Lake. There probably hadn't been a working farm in that area for many years. Luther's Swedish family had settled in the area after the lumber barons moved farther west. Luther left the Drum Lake area to attend one of the state teacher's colleges and did, in fact, become an instructor in the Drum Lake area. Luther left teaching to become the County Agriculture Extension agent and bought a home in Stanleyville. His continuing interest in education led to his running for and winning a seat on the board of trustees. Most of the faculty looked upon him as a champion of "Our Cause," as one who would be fair in dealing with us.

As the years passed it became evident that Luther was not only a fair, honest and simple man, he was also a rather colorful local character. When it was still possible for educational institutions to purchase government surplus, Luther would make periodic trips to the nearest surplus depot in Mansfield about fifty miles to the east. I had the good fortune to be invited on one of these safaris once when the Art Department was in need of tables, stools, counter tops and other odds and ends.

I drove the fifteen miles to Stanleyville and met Luther at his home. Before leaving he had to show me his garage/workshop where he tinkered with many things, including the polishing of a prehistoric Lake Michigan coral known as Petoskey Stones. He made tie clasps and cuff links from the stones. The shop was a wondrous and overpowering area of clutter: the lair of a marvelously individual soul. I was soon beckoned outside where we climbed into Luther's big Buick with a trailer hitched to the rear bumper and began the trip to the surplus depot. Luther had to lean way back in the seat so that his ample stomach cleared the steering wheel. The combination of an early spring frost and just plain dirt across the windshield made it difficult to see much of the road ahead. I was quietly terrified as we went roaring down the highway while Luther sipped on a mug of coffee.

The poor visibility didn't seem to bother Luther much. He'd traveled the little used back roads so often he'd memorized every mile long ago. After the frost had melted I observed that we were driving in some rather lonely and forlorn countryside. When we would pass some long abandoned and crumbling house or barn, Luther would deliver a little history lesson. He seemed to know the last owner of every place we passed as well as the circumstances of the failed dreams each family had once nurtured. He said that most of the families had either gone under during the Depression or immediately following

World War II. Each house had a different story, but most went along the same line. Luther would point to an abandoned home and tell me something like, "See that one? That fella's name was Bellanger. Moved here in the 30's. He tried t' farm the place, but the land was already half played out before he got here. He just up and left in the fall of '48. Nobody's seen 'em since."

On the return from Mansfield, I found out how much of a romantic he really was. He pointed out, on another road, a place he had purchased himself. He'd received a tax break from the state to have the land replanted as a forest and he was hoping to renovate the old 1894 farmhouse and rent it out. To this day I think he just bought it to try and protect at least something in the countryside from complete ruin.

He genuinely wanted to preserve the well-laid wood floors, the marvellous decorative porch spindles and Victorian bric-a-brac in the peaks of the house he had purchased. In a rather somber mood I remember the two of us looking over the place. The house still stood in a mood of dignity despite its long neglected siding. The porch steps had long since become a pile of moist and crumbled wood. The battered screen door flopped helplessly in the wind against the back entrance. In the front yard a dead elm stood silent guard. I glanced at Luther as he described the history of the farmyard and could tell he was quite moved by the vision of this old house and the years of long ago glory.

Luther said that this home had once been the showplace of the southern part of the county. He was really proud to show if off, but he never did receive the joy of seeing it restored. I remember taking many photos of the house, making drawings of its sagging forms and sketching the surrounding, forlorn, landscape. It was really a nostalgic place. Luther often complained that, "Those people from Detroit have poked around and stole all the porcelain door knobs." He would never have accused his neighbors of such a foul deed. I imagined the place was too remote for anyone from Detroit to have had the initiative to search it out.

When Luther returned from one of his forays to the government surplus depot he would have a trailer full of strange and wonderful items he thought might be useful around the campus. On several occasions he would also bring back items that he believed, "folks could use for themselves.": wooden cross-country skis, coils of rope, old army clothing as well as various weird hand tools you'd never find in a local hardware store, such as hand-cranked dowel makers.

When arriving on campus with his loaded trailer Luther would sell the items he had picked out, at cost, to the faculty. After which any extra dollars that were raised would be put into the school's general fund. There was no skimming, no fraud and Luther felt that at least a few tax payers were getting back some of the things they had originally paid for.

When the authorities in Mansfield found out that Luther was selling things back to ordinary citizens he was banned from the depot altogether. He was totally dismayed and so were the rest of us. It was my first contact with what is known in some circles as Bureaucratic Dumbthink. That Luther was treated like a common thief was outrageous to all of us. I considered him a model of honesty and practicality.

Each spring the college hosted an open house for local citizens so they could observe the facilities and parents could meet the people who were educating their children. This included a picnic with food donated by local merchants including buffalo burgers from an experimental farmer nearby.

Luther always attended these open houses and participated by being part of the food serving line, exchanging pleasantries with friend and stranger alike. He always made sure that there were extra benches, tables and chairs, "where," as he'd say, "folks can sit 'n visit."

Luther was a personification of the early folksiness that was promoted at the college in order to keep a close connection with the people. One year, when he was cleaning a large kettle with a bleach solution, he accidentally lowered his tie into the powerful cleaning mixture. Unbeknownst to him, his tie had become faded halfway up. Upon noticing this

Luther announced, with a sheepish grin on his tanned face that, "Mother will have some dye at home and can fix it good as new."

Much to everyone's sadness, Luther retired from the Board of Trustees two years after the faded tie incident because of increasing health problems. A year after his retirement he died. It was a blow to those of us who knew and loved him. Classes were cancelled the afternoon of the funeral and the little Methodist church in Stanleyville was overflowing with mourners. I felt that some of the pompous eulogizing by local dignitaries was an insult to this kind and simple man. Luther had been like a personification of the trusting, hard working and honest Midwestern farmer often depicted in the paintings of Grant Wood, Thomas Hart Benton and John Stewart Curry. After the funeral ended there was a long line of cars heading back to Chippewa Harbor and a group of us gathered at Sladek's. One of my favorite farm boys was no longer with us.

Tessie Garrison's wonderland balustrade with house in the background.

Example of artwork done while exploring the countryside.

Amidst a gathering of friends.

Abandoned rail
tracks and town.

Forlorn and
empty landscape.

A glimpse of the vineyard sage's
grapes and vines.

The "dumb farmers" wishful restoration project.

Author with friend and the t-shirt of choice.

Author's rural homestead.

The parade pranksters unleash the giant vaccum cleaner!

Home of the seminar and Arnie, the folk hero.

The mysterious and haunted Hurley homestead.

Chapter Thirteen
The Beach Party

Some changes never feel right, even when they occur while you're laughing along a beach in the summer. It was not hard to get caught up in the myriad of outdoor activities in the Chippewa Harbor area. One merely had to gaze out into the open waters of North Bay to spot the gently floating sailboats. When passing a nearby stream one could easily understand the opportunities available for trout fishing. We were all aware that at one time Hemingway had lived close by. To me, this area was a Mecca for outdoor fun all year round.

It wasn't long before I discovered one of the Northland's oldest traditions, the beach party. In the 1970's, before the great land rush occurred in northern Michigan, there were seemingly endless miles of open beaches along Lake Michigan and on parts of the harbors and bays that extended inland. Most of the yellow-white sand was clean and the water very clear, each wave cresting would show through like a surreal window to the sand below.

As it turned out the concept of the beach party did not even necessarily require swimming, nor was it absolutely necessary to even conduct such a festivity under the pristine conditions of summer. The main ingredients of the event were collecting people who relished the isolation that could be discovered on a lonely beach, coolers full of beer and protein rich food, as well as a feeling of comradeship and wails of laughter. Often these events became nocturnal adventures, requiring the construction of a large bonfire following a daytime spent gathering driftwood. The beach party would be spent singing hokey rounds along with guitars, reading poetry and limericks, telling ribald jokes, as well as periods of rather engaging conversation. Not to mention spontaneous forays such as late night swimming and group dances beneath a bright and shimmering full moon.

Liz and I, along with our friends, were able to develop our own variations for a beach party. Many of these festive occasions were prearranged to occur on major holidays like Memorial Day, the Fourth of July, as well as Labor Day. The parties, which later became known as treks, were often organized around the appearance of Dan Frazier and Harold Kinard from Lake Huron University. Rather quickly our beach parties became important rituals for us. The parties were a comfortable tradition used to mark, compare and move ahead in our lives together. Occasionally, Dan or Harold would call, outside the framework of the holidays, and indicate a dire need for spiritual renewal, at which time a beach party would be arranged at the soonest possible time. Shortly thereafter we would all load up Harold's van, set out for an isolated beach, giddy and teeming with the kind of free energy and excitement normally observed in young children.

Our beach parties followed an easy and familiar routine. We would start with coolers full of food and drink, blankets to spread across the warm sand, gallons of suntan lotion, cameras, funny hats and large brightly colored towels and shirts. From these standards the parties would proceed in unknown ways.

Like good trout fishing, we couldn't just go off to the very places where everyone else went; we desired to have our beach parties at uncharted spots, away from the crowds. Early on we were given a clue from a local resident and former student, Mary Kratochvil. She informed us that there was an area at the local township park which was habitually ignored by tourists and even the locals. Her advice was correct, we found isolation right before our noses. As a rule, we always avoided the city beaches since they were no more than "Meat Markets" for the youthful beach-side Adonises and sandy-footed Venuses that strutted their sun drenched charms to each other. Sometimes, but rarely, the more daring of these youth even swam, or water skied. The truly athletic dove off the sterns of sailboats.

Our clan looked upon all this with disdain and contempt, perhaps unconsciously repeating phrases we'd heard our parents recite. Anyhow, we all felt superior and became possessive as well, watchful of our tiny township beach paradise. When we would spread our blankets it was as if we were declaring to the world that we would be ourselves no matter what, others should stay away.

There was nothing as exciting as dashing for the cool and refreshing waters of North Bay. Usually while our wives waded along the shoreline looking for Petoskey stones, Harold, Dan and I went for the deep water. It wasn't long before I developed my Great Lake's snobbery. To this day I refuse to swim anywhere I cannot see my feet when the water is up to my chin.

With our area staked out we would swim for hours, performing surface dives, body surfing the waves when they were high. Once, these joyous times were spoiled when Harold hit his nose on a large rock and needed medical attention. As Dan's son grew older, he contributed the frisbee and the beach ball. Both of these items always led to dramatic belly flopping catches in the water. Although these were normally exuberant and high energy outings, I also have fond memories of prolonged and silent moments, all of us in deep thought, listening to the slow and peaceful pulse of the waves and the haunting cry of sea gulls overhead.

Many times, following hours of energetic cavorting, the beach party would be moved back to our house where Harold would perform his magic on the grill. After good food and normally too much wine, a deep and peaceful feeling would capture us all. Such warm memories continue to endure. The Labor Day beach treks were always bittersweet, as they signaled the rapid approach of a new school year and the coming of the long winter.

One of the most memorable beach parties was not our creation, but the product of a rather restless and troubled man named Donovan Bradley. Donovan was an instructor in the Philosophy Department at the College, his speciality was nineteenth century logic and epistemology. Donovan arrived on campus a year after I did and since we were both graduates of Southern Michigan University, knew many of the same people. This led me to introduce him to Harold and Dan. From time to time Donovan would join us in revelry.

Donovan was a slightly built fellow, who spoke in a quiet monotone that was rather difficult to understand. In Sladek's, on a Friday evening he was all but drowned out by the background noise, yet he would continue to speak in philosophical circles anyway.

Donovan also had an appreciation of the arts, but most importantly, he possessed a rather offbeat sense of humor and a fertile imagination. One of the first signs of this was his creation of the Edna D. Stanton Memorial Motorcycle Club, which was formed in honor of a long dead and very obscure Michigan poet buried in nearby Mansfield. This club consisted of making a pilgrimage to the grave side of Edna Stanton. The first voyage consisted of two motorcycles and two vans. Those of us who attended performed a mock grave side tribute which was then followed by a picnic and the reading of some of Edna Stanton's poetry. The event was quite lively since we all wore t-shirts that had been made for the event and displayed the dramatic banners we'd made all around Ms. Stanton's grave site. Donovan talked on and on about how we should create a letterhead and how we must all lobby for a state holiday on Ms. Stanton's behalf. We championed each new idea presented with jolts of loud cheer.

Unfortunately only one run was made to honor Edna Stanton. One reason no other runs were made to the grave site of Mrs. Stanton was that Donovan's motorcycle was repossessed. The

Memorial Motorcycle Club could hardly continue if its leader had no cycle.

As the years passed, Donovan would frequently inquire as to when my friends from Lake Huron University would be coming to town. Over time, though, Dan and Harold became a bit wary of contact with Donovan because of what they had begun to sense was the Midas Touch in reverse. It seemed that most of what Donovan got involved with turned to junk: the short-lived motorcycle club and his tempestuous relationships, to wrecked cars and unpaid bills.

Donovan's bad luck culminated about eight years after he moved to town. As usual everything started with a golden opportunity though. After renting a series of dingy apartments and tiny rooms Donovan discovered a beach house that was up for rent. He quickly rented the house and intended to host his own beach parties. At first our clan attended some of Donovan's beach parties, yet we all seemed to agree that there was something missing in the atmosphere and tone. The parties seemed almost morose, as if attended by ghosts and vacant spirits.

After a few of Donovan's parties, our wives refused to attend. Donovan was a sort of magnet for every misfit in the county. There were often unpublished authors milling about, frustrated poets, seldom heard musicians, as well as a consistent clustering of just plainly defeated individuals. All too often it seemed that people thought the isolation and forested hills of the north would somehow allow for a new life, but rarely did easy and miraculous prosperity occur, which in turn seemed to promote even more feelings of despair.

Although the beach house came along as a magnificent haven, it soon started to slip. The interior walls seemed to close in. When the sun would set, the house became a scene of gloom and despair, crisscrossing shadows filtered at odd angles, yellowed roller blinds flapped and ripped during light breezes. Donovan's Uncle broke his leg when he slipped on a crumbling concrete step and the water pipes had burst and flooded the house one winter morning creating a sheet of ice. Then when spring arrived the same water left a moldy and unpleasant smell. Just as Dan and Harold expected, the Donovan jinx seemed to be thriving.

Sometime near the end of the seventies, during the always bittersweet holiday of Labor Day, Donovan's beach parties came to an end. Early in August, Donovan communicated to me that he would be hosting a large beach party and wanted me and my friends to attend.

That evening, I called Harold Kinard. After a few opening pleasantries, I said, "Say there; ol' Sport, I encountered Donovan today and he wants me to invite you and Dan to what he claims will be a wondrous gathering at this beach-side Shangri-la Labor Day weekend."

"Oh really," Harold began softly chuckling, and then added, "We haven't been up in a long time and it is Labor Day, this sounds like it could be a good show. Jane and I will be there. I think Ben Longstreet, a former student, would like to see one of these beach fiascoes too. You remember Ben don't you?"

I replied that I did, "By all means bring Ben if he doesn't mind the old couch on the sun porch as sleeping quarters. Remember to call Dan and Sue."

An hour later Harold called back and announced that everyone was eager to come.

As it turned out, Ben had developed a curiosity for Donovan's unusual parties through Harold's descriptions and wanted to see one for himself.

Harold, Dan and the others arrived in a festive mood the night before the grand event at Donovan's. The next morning, to avoid any abandonment of our own traditions, we planned appropriately. Over one of Dan's famous, large country breakfasts it was decided that none of us wished to spend the entire day at Donovan's so we decided to put together our own beach party prior.

Sometime, amidst our own beach party that day, someone remembered that we needed to pack up and go. After all, we didn't want to miss Donovan's grand attempt at a beach party. As we slowly packed up, to my complete surprise, Liz and Sue Frazier expressed an interest in going with us. Jane Kinard opted for more tranquility and was dropped off at our house.

When we arrived at the edge of Donovan's beach we noticed a healthy collection of cars scattered about his yard and along the road. Parking our car we located the path to Donovan's beach house. There were about forty people sitting and milling around. Some were on blankets, some were standing, one small group was tossing a frisbee in what seemed slow motion and maybe two or three other people were ankle deep in the water. Everyone was silent and separate, there seemed to be no sense of festivity. Conversation was at a bare and muted minimum.

To avoid this scene we spread our blankets away from the house and the beach so that we could simply watch this sleepy drama unfold before us. Shortly after our arrival, a metallic gold speedboat appeared on the horizon of North Bay and glided up to the shore. Dan and Harold glanced at each other and rolled their eyes. It was Lance Brunner and his cousin, Bruce. These guys were in their mid-thirties and had brought along two teenage, bikini-clad, nymphettes who giggled and self-consciously clung together while Lance and his cousin attempted to show off the young girls as trophies. These two men were both well built and tanned from long exposure to the elements, but there was something sinister and unholy about their masculinity. Neither of these men was well-liked, and they had very few friends who could tolerate them. They were considered by all as ultra-narcissistic, even violent.

As we watched all of this rather bizarre role-playing enacted before us, Ben asked if I would take him inside the beach house so that he could see if it was as strange in there as it was outside. Strolling over in silence, we entered the headquarters of this party and found a cache of zombies inside the beach house. One of the guests was a member of Donovan's short lived motorcycle club who slowly nodded when we came in. Upon seeing that this scene was yet another dead end, Ben and I returned to our blanket sanctuary. Ben declared to Harold, "My God, I didn't believe you guys when you told me about these parties. This Donovan guy breeds boredom!"

We all felt sorry for Donovan in a way. It seemed unfortunate that he would never be able to experience the excitement of a beach party.

As we sat shaking our heads in disbelief over Donovan's party, Dan's laughter still in the air, the fatal end arrived. Not just for Donovan's party, but, in my mind, the entire tradition of the beach party itself.

From behind Donovan's beach house, clattering down the gentle slope was the crashing, growling and clanking noise of a Goliath-sized bulldozer. This frightful machine began to destroy the beach grass, crush willow trees and level out the sandy mounds beside Donovan's rental property. The lifeless guests were startled into action, taking cover.

They were joined by a family of mallard ducks who hastily waddled to safety.

Glaring at the bulldozer I sensed that although the machine operator was somewhat ashamed at first, as he watched the frightened people scatter, he began enjoying himself. Donovan emerged from his beach house and was visibly shaken, but admitted to those around him that most of the beach was owned by a newly formed residential association across the road and up in the hills. He declared he truly had no recourse to halt the machine. The party would have to be moved. Naturally, it wasn't long before his guests began to leave.

I had consumed enough beer to have my courage inflated and my Balkan temper aroused. "DAN!" I declared, "Let's knock that guy off that damn machine and drive it right out in the middle of the bay!

Dan was a sturdily built fellow who never ran from a scuffle, but he showed timely restraint by firmly grasping my shoulder and saying, "Easy, Jack, easy now. They'd have a new dozer here on Monday and we'd all be in jail."

Dan brought me back to a more realistic position on this disastrous situation. Dan also went on to surmise that, since it was Saturday, this tactless act was costing the owners a pretty penny and would make my ambush idea even more costly if followed through. It was clear to us that this was a hostile act of elitist arrogance. The new housing association seemed to be trying to teach some sort of obtuse lesson that Donovan and his type of guests and activities weren't welcome on, or near, THEIR beach any longer. They seemed to assume they had some right to make these beaches conform with their sense of what was right. These people wanted a Hollywood beach, not the bramble and ducks and stones that to us made the area interesting. It seemed obvious that the association members had decided that because they had money they could do what they wanted, remaking this beach into a phony paradise for themselves and their spoiled children.

We did feel that if we wanted to complain about this destruction, we might have had a legitimate legal stance, but instead the whole event seemed a dark omen of what was to become of the land and mind frame of the region.

The following year, Donovan abandoned the idea of the beach party and purchased a home away from the water on a heavily wooded lot. By this time, beach front property was beginning to be priced out of the range many of the local residents could afford anyway.

Donovan was finally able to get the last laugh on us though. When the college announced an early retirement plan for faculty and staff, Donovan cleverly pieced together a retirement plan of previous military service and several state jobs to add to his years spent teaching and was one of the first to depart from the teaching ranks. After his last graduation ceremony, we all watched him with thinly disguised envy as he confidently jumped in his car and left the parking lot for a new life of his own.

My group of friends continued to engage in beach parties after the bulldozer disaster at Donovan's. However the memory of this day dampened our tradition in a slow and somber way. Over time, an activity that was intended to be one of simple enjoyment and frolic had become less pure and even unwelcome in the eyes of the changing society around us.

Chapter Fourteen
Elections, Pancakes
And Junk

Many local activities in the area could have easily been labeled social institutions during my years in Chippewa Harbor. However, some events were revered and participated in with stronger dedication and regularity than others.

One of these social rituals was certainly any Election Day, whether it be a local primary election, or national election, especially in the days before the avalanche many of us came to know as the population explosion in North Bay Township. If the polls were not crowded, one often cast their ballot quickly, with just a few easy words to the people working the tables where registrations were checked. The same gentle faces would often work these tables for years and eventually a person was able to become friendly with them. These people didn't seem to have the looks of boredom you often see on polling place volunteers today, perhaps apathetic voting turnouts have something to do with this.

The polling places in North Bay Township were usually quite crowded though, whether it was at the old township hall, or at the new fire station that was built nearby. When waiting in line people would become engaged in conversation. Election days presented an ideal opportunity to catch up with nearby neighbors. This seemed especially true of the more remote farmers in the area, who, after casting their votes, after participating in the democracy we all cherished, would form a small pack outside to discuss the issues at hand. These men always seemed careful to speak in hushed tones, as if trying not to influence anyone still headed inside to vote.

Another occasion that brought the township residents out in droves was the annual Volunteer Fire Department Pancake Breakfast. This event was always relished as a social gathering since it was an opportunity to feast heartily on pancakes, sausage and scrambled eggs, all of which was then washed down with flagons of hot, strong coffee, then topped with a few rounds of sugar dusted donuts. All of these culinary wonders were prepared by the broadly smiling, rosy cheeked wives of the noble and courageous fire fighting volunteers. In the early days of our residency, the fire fighting force was made up of farmers and other men who held laboring jobs within the township limits. If you worked in town you wouldn't always be available when smoke appeared on the horizon, and thus not eligible to participate.

Along with eating one's fill at these opulent events, there was always the chance to meet new people and widen your circle of acquaintances which, in turn, made you feel like you were beginning to fit into the rather complex social fabric of the township. There was also the good feeling you had of contributing your ticket price toward the general well-being and maintenance of the fire department's buildings and equipment. I was always proud to contribute to the township community, especially as I got to know the region and people around me.

One of the more important and unexpected glues that held North Bay together turned out to be the township dump. I have no clue when this hallowed place was created, but it must have been when nonagricultural residents began filtering in, or as when influential, longtime summer residents began to tire of dumping their trash in the low spots on their own land.

Another theory came from Ellie and Ed Weaver who over the years of operating their orchard had heard a different version about the beginnings of the dump. Ellie told me that the dump was partially created because of the large numbers of mink ranches. She recalled that shortly after World War II a number of the township fruit growers decided to raise mink on the side in order to augment their incomes. She also remembered the problems that these mink ranches created. For instance her dogs and cats began to return to her house with dead mink in their mouths. Also, mink that escaped the cages at the ranches began to roam freely and soon competed with the raccoons in foraging and generally making a mess throughout the township. Every place trash was spread, in crevices and ditches through the township, soon became nesting and exploration grounds for the escaped mink. Of course the waste by-products from these mink ranches was a complete ecological disaster as well, especially when simply laid out in the open. The mink farms, according to Ellie, really required a more centralized location for disposal. Thus, the mink menace, coupled with pressure from the nonagricultural residents for a reasonable way to dispose of garbage, seems to have led to the opening of the township dump which was paid for and used by everyone.

The dream of riches through raising mink only lasted a few years in the township. The market for these pelts never really became the money maker as hoped and so many a farmer's dream evaporated.

When we first moved into our beloved farmhouse, we started out keeping the trash pickup service used by the previous owners. One day though, when mentioning this to our neighbor, Mr. Novotny, I was told that we could save some money by taking our trash to the township dump. Mr. Novotny also pointed out that if we ever had any heavy duty appliances to get rid of, perhaps a deceased water heater, or defunct refrigerator, the roadside pickup service wouldn't help. He happily gave me directions to the township dump and a week later I made my first journey to what soon become a strangely enchanting spot for me.

Liz and I carefully bagged our kitchen scraps, any paper not used in the fireplace, as well as other odds and ends, then loaded the back of the station wagon for my maiden trip to the dump. I drove north on our main road, took the left turn a mile past the township hall, then, as instructed, went down the first left past the old school house onto Satan's Slide Road, appropriately named for its steep and twisting grade. I was warned not to go too far, or the road would take me right into some farmer's yard. Carefully watching for the dump site, I found that it was clearly marked, denoted with both a sign and chain link fence that went around three sides, enclosing perhaps an acre and a half of land, nestled partially amidst the steep slope of Satan's slide. I drove in to the dump and stopped at what I assumed was the keeper's shanty.

The keeper's name was Charlie Boyd. He was a tall, slender fellow with long, curly hair and a scruffy beard. He emerged from the shanty wearing army fatigues and I half expected there to be a secret password, or handshake for admittance. Strains of classical music drifted out the open door of the shanty when he came forth to meet me. A quick glance inside his hut revealed an oriental rug across the floor. He waved me out of the car, pointing me to go to the rear of my car.

While I went to the rear of our station wagon to swing open the door, my eyes were quickly drawn to the side of the shanty. It was covered with discarded picture frames, paintings and pictures. Out a little beyond the north wall of the shanty were four tall cedar poles reaching skyward. All up and down these tall poles were wooden pegs, jutting out at various angles. On these pegs Charlie had hung an odd assortment of objects, such as bicycle tires, children's toys, kitchen utensils and cook ware, coils of rope and wire, even spare parts for baby carriages. The variety of items on display was staggering. The whole scene appeared as four blessed totem poles with offerings for some strange and esoteric god above.

As I stood there in utter bewilderment, I was suddenly aware again of Charlie's presence. His voice cut through the fog I was in, "Three bags, not too much weight, that'll be a buck I guess." As I fumbled around in my wallet I noticed that Charlie had pitched my bags down a chute to a giant dumpster down below.

As I drove away from the shanty and turned to exit, I noticed that along the perimeter of the township dump was where the heavy stuff was being discarded. There among the rust and weeds laid the remaining hulks of kitchen stoves and washers, items no longer able to provide the heat, or comfort required from those of us in the township.

Upon my arrival back home, I burst through the back door and into the kitchen where Liz was wrestling with a large bowl of cookie dough. I began to clamor, "Geez, Dear, what a place! The caretaker mounts things on poles like some surreal museum. He plays classical music while tossing trash. I've never seen anything like this!"

Liz replied, "Oh Jack, you get excited over the most bizarre things, this is just another of your embellished stories."

"NO, No, no," I protested, "It's like a rust covered fairy land." My excited babble went unheeded as Liz continued dropping blobs of cookie dough on shiny baking sheets. I walked away moping that my wondrous discovery had been treated as just another half-baked fantasy.

Even though Liz imagined I was nuts, I knew this rusty wonderland needed further research, so I consulted both the Weavers and Novotnys. I learned that Charlie's way of decorating the dump was his original approach at recycling. Any item that he felt had not lost its usefulness was hung on the wall, or the poles and anyone wishing to take them home was welcome to do so. When something was removed the empty slot was quickly filled with yet another of Charlie's recycled wonders. I discovered and agreed that Charlie was one of the township's true eccentrics. His eccentric aura was strengthened by the fact that neither I, nor anyone I knew ever saw Charlie anywhere but at the dump. How, or where he stocked up on food, got his clothing, or what he did for entertainment remained a mystery to us all. It was mildly rumored that he made a valiant and clear, pink rhubarb wine.

I also discovered that Charlie would allow anyone, any adult that is, to poke around in the graveyard of appliances. One day, after tossing some scrap galvanized piping into this collage of junk, I noticed that someone had tossed away a railroad crossing sign. As I drove home, I got the idea of salvaging this treasure and placing it upright at the end of our long driveway. I decided that I would return the next day and brave the tangle of plumbing pipes and other junk to retrieve this sign.

Returning the next day, my burning enthusiasm was snuffed out when I discovered that someone had beaten me to it.

Quite depressed, I parked my car and trudged up to Charlie's shanty. As I neared his residence I could hear Beethoven's *Ninth Symphony* drifting through the air. I stuck my head in the door and asked, "Hey, Charlie, did you see anyone carry off an old railroad crossing sign? I know I saw one yesterday under that pile of old pipe."

Charlie's startled eyes peered at me from under his fatigue cap. "Well, ah, ... I dunno. There was a fella in an old truck poking around yesterday. He must've taken it."

Over the years it slowly became obvious to me how the dump functioned as a social institution. If one arrived at a time when the giant dumpster was being changed, or if there was a line, or even a cluster of folks discussing an item in the collage of junk, a person was inclined to engage in conversation. Some of the stories of the discarded junk verged on social history. From time to time one could observe two, three, or even four men leaning on the hood of a car, or the fender of a pickup truck sharing a good natured story, or catching up on some news around the township. Delays of any sort at the dump were not the makings of Charlie though, he liked to keep the cars moving along as best he could.

Having passed through several stages of life, many times I've fantasized about freezing periods of time when life was good, when experiences were plentiful and rewarding, but alas, this can never happen. Change is unavoidable even for the most beloved people and places. The transitions of life have altered the township dump as well.

The first sign of a changed life-style at the dump occurred as the population began to swell in the area. A sign of this influx of new people and a lack of appreciation for the area occurred about two years after our departure from the township.

Someone must have noticed that at day's end, Charlie always had large amounts of cash around the shanty and decided to rob him at gunpoint. Soon thereafter, one needed a monthly punch card to use the dump, no cash was to be used on the spot. After this unforgivable crime was committed, Charlie was relieved of his duties as Dump Baron because some simpleton, in a place of power and who had probably never even been to the dump, decided that Charlie was overly involved with fermented beverages and that his personal habits would somehow interfere with his efficiency. No account was taken that Charlie had already proved himself quite capable of maintaining the dump for years and years. Then, because of the fear of a lawsuit, the township prohibited scavenging amid the tangles of heavy junk. Gone as well were Charlie's totem's to the high spirits of the sky and his shanty wall art collection. One can only hope that Charlie's totem pole offerings will somehow be resurrected.

CHAPTER FIFTEEN
BUDDIES & SIDEKICKS

Many of us have encountered the joy of having a unique friend, such as when two men, or two women form such a strong bond of friendship, they seem to become inseparable. In literature for instance, my first memory of this bond was with Sancho Panza and Don Quixote. This combination left a strong impression on me. Sancho Panza was practical and realistic while Don Quixote was a complete romantic and dreamer. Together they were able to balance each other, living out a sort of separate life from normal society. Sancho would often need to venture into the dream world in order to rescue Quixote from moments of extreme romanticism. I can remember as well, from Hollywood, Roy Rogers and Gene Autry, each of whom appeared with a trusty sidekick that was to provide some sort of comic relief. The sidekicks were always more than just comic, however, they would also support the hero and save him from any impending peril. The real purpose of these hero sidekicks always seemed to demonstrate the importance and value of loyalty, as well as the meaning of trustworthiness and dependability through companionship. The moral to a certain extent became that any peril might be overcome when friends could rely on each other for support.

In my own right, while in Chippewa Harbor, I was lucky to develop a loyal friendship with Freddie Bates. Although neither of us seemed to take on the hero role, we did share a strong bond and the ability, from time to time, to get each other out of trouble. Early on we discovered we had similar interests, especially drawing and exploring the local landscape. We both seemed to be working at our landscape art in the same way. Our similarities and portrayals seemed unconsciously alike even though we talked very little about what we were doing. At times we appeared to be thinking as one person. Each of us found this a rather challenging and amazing situation.

Early on we both began to meet and know some of the local fruit growers. Freddie had managed to rent a house in the country, surrounded by fruit orchards, from one of the local growers. This allowed us an easy way to venture out in all directions and develop our efforts at landscape art.

On a radiant and brilliant autumn day, with charcoal pencils and drawing paper in hand, Freddie and I were exploring the views around the orchards of Adam Novotny, the brother of my neighbor, when we stumbled upon what appeared to be an abandoned and neglected grape arbor. Since we had both become interested and skilled at winemaking, this was clearly an unfair temptation placed in front of us.

We briefly considered this a sign from some compassionate God who was working on our behalf. Before we could take this idea too far, Freddie came up with some quick witted joke and stirred us back to reality and the situation at hand. We hastily returned to Freddie's house, grabbed grocery sacks and returned for the coveted grapes. Busily picking as many grapes as possible, thoughts of red wine tumbling through our brains, we believed we were the luckiest two fellows alive. The next day we set out to crushing and stamping the grapes for what was to be a truly regal batch of red wine.

It was a few days later, when we met Adam himself while he was out inspecting his orchard. The two of us waved and walked over to Adam for a chat. As the three of us stood around talking, Adam suddenly mentioned, "Funniest thing, I was headed down yesterday to the woods there to pick some of them grapes and there wasn't hardly any there, 'coons must've got 'em. Boy, was my wife disappointed, Mother always makes a batch of jam about this time of year."

Freddie and I glanced at each other momentarily while our stomachs sunk to our knees. We realized that we hadn't found an abandoned treasure trove, but had inadvertently taken from this family's table a year's supply of grape jelly. We felt pretty foolish. Yet, at the same time, it was impossible to admit our shortcomings so we both solemnly agreed with Adam that, yes, the raccoons must have gotten them.

Both Freddie and I became avid cross country skiers as well. During the winter months, we would gather at his rented farm house and venture out amidst the rolling hills. Many times our wives would start out following us, but getting tired or more likely, expressing rational judgment, return early to the warm house and tumblers full of hot spiced cider. Their departure would leave Freddie and me free to more maniacal feats which almost always involved high speed, grand jumps and, in our wives' minds, decisions based on all-around stupidity. It was normal for us to race down the razorback hills barely missing slightly buried barbed wire fences or cruising with banzai cries between cherry trees until we both found our faces planted in the snow, at which point we would break out in rippling shouts of joy. The thrill of the moment would always capture both of us. We shared an attraction to this same type of excitement.

Freddie and I also shared, as good friends do, our personal joys and sorrows. Whenever each of us needed help, the other would provide relief, from helping with furniture being moved to listening and trying to solve personal problems which might arise. When Freddie and his wife were divorced, Liz and I were very watchful to include him in all of our social events at the house. Since he was well acquainted with my other good friends, Harold and Dan, he was always comfortable and expected to join us in any sort of madcap revelry that we generated.

Whenever there was an opening for an art exhibition Freddie would accompany us. In fact, we sort of became a sideshow at the openings in town. One of us would take on the straight man, the other the jester, building jokes and laughter for all who cared to listen, often driving the serious artists out the door. We merged at these parties into a sort of third character. Just as our jokes and winemaking have prospered over time, our friendship has endured over the years as well.

Perhaps even more outstanding than my friendship with Freddie was another dynamic duo comprised of Doctor Samuel Ashcroft and his Falstaffian sidekick Jerry Dobbins. The good Doctor Ashcroft was a tall, slender and distinguished man with dark wavy hair and a neatly trimmed beard. He carried himself in a stately manner with a straight back and a sense of self-assuredness.

Jerry Dobbins, on the other hand, was a short, stout, barrel-like man with strong arms and shoulders, topped off with a wide, round cherubic face to which was attached a somewhat unruly handlebar mustache. He was always blunt and spoke with a hoarse and raspy voice which sounded like gravel stirring in a cement truck.

The first time I encountered these two together, I was reminded of Quixote and Panza. Doctor Sam, although a brilliant surgeon, was prone to vanishing into his dreams. He would break away from conversation daydreaming about extravagant fishing gear, or about some day meeting the lady of his dreams. At times like these, as the perfect sidekick ought to do, Jerry Dobbins would sit Doctor Sam down and with severe bluntness and precision, bring the Doctor back to reality.

My initial encounter with Doctor Sam was set up through a visit I had to make to the Doctor's office. I had burst some tendons in my right arm, a common enough injury up in the Northwoods, while cutting firewood. It was during the return trips I made to his office to monitor my recovery that the two of us began to converse and engage in small talk. During one of these checkups, I informed Doctor

Sam that I was an enthusiastic wine maker. Upon learning this the Doctor's face lit up and he explained his tastes in wines. This was the first time I saw the Doctor vanish into his dream-like state of being.

A few weeks after we had spoken of wine, I ran across Doctor Sam again while catching up on some errands around town. After a few minutes of chitchat, Doctor Sam's eyes resumed his dreamy glaze and he began to describe in great relish the wonderful dinner he and Jerry had eaten at the Whispering Pines Lodge the night before. The meal sounded fascinating to me. It was full of fine delicacies: caviar and lobster, all of which had been complemented with a rousingly successful bottle of white Bordeaux picked out by Jerry. As Doctor Sam explained all of this I understood that Doctor Sam was a complete *bon vivant*. It became clear that he and Jerry put a great deal of energy into the pursuit of the "good life."

After Doctor Sam finished his colorful description of the meal he smiled, looked at me a moment and then with a burst of spontaneous enthusiasm suggested, "Say, why don't you join us sometime Jack? We could really have a lot of fun!"

I nodded and agreed most assuredly it would be a lot of fun. "I'd love an evening out on the town. Two weeks from tomorrow my wife is going to Nebraska to help with her cousin's fledgling political campaign. He's running for the legislature I think.

We're all excited for him and my wife wants to provide some additional help in the closing weeks."

To this Doctor Sam said, "Wonderful. I know just the time for us to meet, two weeks from this Friday. Why don't you meet Jerry and me at the Whispering Pines Lodge dining room at six o'clock?"

Not wanting to miss this opportunity I agreed and indicated I would see them soon.

The day before the appointed dinner, I had taken my wife to the airport and with the prospects of a month of bachelorhood, became quite anxious for the next day's adventure with Doctor Sam and Jerry.

As the time for the dinner arrived, I dressed in slightly better clothing than I normally would for an evening out and arrived in the parking lot of the Whispering Pines at the appointed time. As I entered the spacious dining room and approached the lobby, I was greeted by a charming lady who quietly and politely said to me, "Oh, you must be Jack. Doctor Sam is waiting for you at his normal table around the backside." As I rounded the corner, there sat Doctor Sam with a gruff looking man I learned was Jerry Dobbins. As soon as Doctor Sam saw me he smiled eagerly, waved and beckoned me on over, gleefully saying, "Hi there Jack, glad you could make it tonight. We're really going to enjoy things this evening. Say, let me introduce you to Jerry Dobbins."

Jerry stood up, reached out a strong hand, grabbed mine and uttered, "Glad tah meetcha Jack."

Doctor Sam said, "We were just having a cocktail. What would you like?"

"Ahh, a vodka martini sounds really good right now," I said.

Sam waved the waiter over, placed my order and ordered another cocktail for each of them. As I sat there looking at the fancy decor of the dining room, I thought to myself, "Thank God it's pay day, a lot of money will be going down the tubes here tonight."

The waiter returned with drinks and then I was presented with a menu. I looked at the menu with a mixture of excitement and suspicion. Although it was the seventies, the menu seemed to be an indicator of times to come. There was certainly nothing on the menu I could afford. I was flabbergasted and, momentarily, quite disappointed. Doctor Sam must have sensed my fleeting gloom and cheerily said to me, "Don't worry Jack, order whatever you like. Jerry and I are going to pick up the bill."

I protested and tried to indicate that they needn't do that, but Jerry waved his hand and declared in his hoarse and curt voice, "Ahhhh, just sit back and enjoy yerself, Jack!"

Finally after some deliberation and discussion about food and chefs and seasonings, we all made our decisions. I would have been quite pleased with anything on the menu, but finally selected a Berlin-style Chicken Fricassee with a side dish of Bavarian red cabbage. Jerry ordered braised lamb and eggplant while Doctor Sam ordered Venison tenderloin in brandy sauce.

After making our decisions, Jerry indicated that, "delicacies like this can't be washed down with water," raised his arm and informed the waiter that we would like a good bottle of Merlot and their best white Bordeaux.

As I sat listening and observing these two, I shortly learned that they had both been recently divorced. I decided that if they couldn't fill their hearts then at least they could fill their stomachs.

During the course of this feast, I asked Jerry what he did for a living. He informed me he owned a saw mill up in Benedict County and did custom lumbering and tree cutting. It turned out we had each met Doctor Sam under similar circumstances. He had been laid out with a logging accident. Jerry explained that custom timber cutting was only done in summer, spring and fall. During the winter he dabbled in the sale of antiques. Then, in a slightly more bitter tone, Jerry explained that for years he had performed his timber cutting business alone, but now he employed his brother who had been a commercial fisherman. At this point Jerry became quite obviously upset, slapping his hand on the table, lightly shaking the silverware.

He went on, "When I was young there were four or five boats that sailed out of Dunbar harbor in the morning! My brother George was one of them until those jackasses at the state capital caved in to sport fishing lobbies and took most of the commercial fishers off the lake!" To emphasize this point, Jerry rammed his fist down on the table harder than before, sending all the silverware and plates clattering and ringing. Then he said, "Now, only the Peterson's are left! Not only that, the damn state only left them a postage stamp sized area to fish in. Why can't the state understand the Great Lakes could be a food source for the whole upper Midwest."

Doctor Sam, between bites of food, agreed with Jerry, saying, "You ought to see some of those so-called sportsmen. They're always fighting for spots along the rivers. Why, they even fight over the fish they've already caught. Not any of them deserve the privilege of fishing at all."

As the dinner continued, serious conversation seemed to slow down as the consumption of food increased. More good hearted conversation occurred instead, mainly commentary on fine foods and offhand jokes about wine making and women. I noticed that when Jerry laughed, his whole body would shake and that even the legs on the chair he sat in teetered back and forth. When we had all finished our main course, we sat in contentment for a few moments. Then Doctor Sam, with an air of confidence, motioned to the waiter and ordered Cherries Jubilee for all of us. This wonderful, flaming dessert was then followed with cognac, coffee and exceptional cigars.

At that moment I felt completely immersed in the "good life" which these two men pursued. As we left the dining room, I thanked both of them profusely for the evening of gourmet delights and luxury. I drove home in a state of bliss.

After the conversation at the Whispering Pines that evening, I was mildly surprised to find that Doctor Sam was a sports fisherman himself. About a month after my dinner with Jerry and Doctor Sam, I was invited to join them for a day aboard the Doctor's boat, the *Ruthie Lee*, which was moored at the large city dock.

When I arrived Jerry and Doctor Sam were awaiting my arrival. They stood aboard the *Ruthie Lee* which appeared to be an old Coast Guard supply boat about twenty feet long. The hull was dark-green with a funny looking cracker box cabin painted a rather gingerly peeling, sage green. When I hopped aboard, the engine was fired up and off we chugged into the waters of North Bay. The further out we went, the more dreamy Doctor Sam became. He was obviously charmed with the water and the prospects of fish. He had four brackets to attach fishing rods to and began earnestly to inspect his fishing radars.

I was not as interested in the water and the fish as I was about the view of the landscape. The lay of the land, the hills, the greenery and reflections of the land formations were marvelous to me. I felt somewhat dreamy, like Doctor Sam, as I viewed the majestic landscape of northern Michigan. That day we ended up talking more about wine and food than fishing. A strong wind and a rising barometric pressure, explained Doctor Sam, probably caused the fish to go into hiding. Upon our return he promised we would catch fish the next time out.

My next voyage out in the *Ruthie Lee* occurred while my wife's parents were in town. Not always comfortable with planning activities with my father-in-law, Doctor Sam saved the day. My father-in-law and I were invited by Doctor Sam to go on a fishing trip. This offer was graciously accepted and a time to meet set up. My father-in-law, being from the Great Plains, was not accustomed to such large bodies of water and looked upon this outing with great zest.

We arrived for the day's great adventure around seven in the morning. As I had become accustomed to seeing them, there stood Jerry and Doctor Sam, anxiously awaiting our arrival, all grins and handshakes. They were going to provide us with a morning of fun and adventure as we chased the wily lake trout. The day was glimmering with October light and the landscape shone with the early morning's level sunlight as if diamonds and jewels. All of the sudden, while we were moving along through the bay, Doctor Sam, peering into his fish radar, declared, "A-ha men! There they are, just to the left." Doctor Sam quickly began cranking the steering wheel, turning the boat sharply to the left.

Jerry stood at the stern of the boat, manning the four fishing lines. He was his usual stout self, with his trademark stubby cigar cornered in his mouth. As Doctor Sam turned the boat, Jerry stammered with as much volume as his raspy voice could muster, "Fer' God's Sake Sam, don't turn her too sharp, you'll foul all the damn lines!"

No straightening of the boat occurred, but as Doctor Sam finished his turn and the boat straightened out, Jerry whooped that they had one on the line then another and another and yet another. As if a gift from the underwater world, we were suddenly able to battle and pull in four vividly colored lake trout. My father-in-law was extremely pleased, pulling a couple of them in himself. With the sun high in the sky, we returned to the dock. Doctor Sam and Jerry unsparingly bestowed the four large fish upon us.

With smiles of great satisfaction, the four of us parted company with another round of handshakes and waves. My father-in-law and I returned home immediately to clean and prepare the fish for lunch. There is no taste to rival the flavors of trout eaten within a few hours after being caught. There was no mistake, Doctor Sam and Jerry's generosity had provided us with a memorable and exciting adventure.

In addition to fine dining in town and ventures out on to the waters of North Bay, Doctor Sam and Jerry were notorious for their occasional parties at Doctor Sam's somewhat remote house in the woods along the shore of North Bay. These parties were carefully planned and attended by only a few selected friends at a time. These events had an aura of mystery and decadence surrounding them and it wasn't long before Freddie and I were invited to one a few months after my trip out to the bay with my father-in-law.

My friend Freddie had become a friend of Doctor Sam and Jerry's too, primarily because of his winemaking abilities and sense of humor, which both Doctor Sam and Jerry enjoyed.

Freddie and I were both informed that we were to bring along the best homemade wine from our cellars which included rhubarb, cherry and a variety of red grape wines. At this time I had also come into the ownership of a small laboratory still through which I would run my punk wines, producing very interesting and highly potent varieties of brandy. When I informed Doctor Sam of this invention, he was quite pleased with me and believed I had made a grand contribution to the development of mankind.

Doctor Sam informed me, as well, that Jerry had just devised a homemade still himself out of an old pressure cooker and some copper tubing, but had not tried it yet. I was asked if I could bring along any reject wine for the christening of Jerry's distillery. I informed Doctor Sam that I did, in fact, have two gallons of cherry wine I would bring. This would allow an attempt to produce some homemade cherry brandy called Kirsch. The prospect of this was grandly approved over the phone by Doctor Sam.

Doctor Sam's home in the woods was about four to five miles north of our home on Westshore Road. Freddie and I were instructed to arrive in the late afternoon. As I gathered up the wine, as well as the two gallons of punk cherry wine and prepared to leave, Liz stood in the doorway and yelled out a stream of instructions for me follow.

"Don't stay too late, don't drink too much and try to be careful!" I nodded my head and went on to explain, as any good husband would, that there would be no problems and, in fact, I believed I would even be home at an early hour.

As I pulled into Doctor Sam's driveway, Jerry waddled out to greet me and shook my hand in gruff fashion. I handed Jerry my bag containing the wine I had brought and asked if he'd carry this in for me. I would carry the precious cargo of punk cherry wine to use in his still. Jerry looked at the wine and grinned. "Can't wait to try it," he uttered.

As we entered the cabin, Jerry set my table wine down and I followed him to the still. "Pour it right in the cooker, Jack!" Jerry ordered. A gleam of great anticipation crossed his broad face. I poured the wine in.

"Let's fire 'er up and get it started!" Jerry proclaimed.

A roar of approval arose from the dining area where all the other men were assembled. I recognized Freddie's laugh.

Freddie and I stood together and examined Jerry's still. Protruding from the lid of the cooker was a coil of copper tubing which Jerry had rigged up to run through a pan of ice cubes and then over the side of the sink toward the floor where a flask had been placed to receive the finished product. The wine was to be brought almost to a boil, then the heat would be turned down, the lid securely fastened and the tubing affixed above. After he lit the fire, Jerry had an eager audience. All of us were anxious to taste the first few drops as soon as they appeared. It would be a while longer Jerry explained. Miracles took time we all philosophically agreed in unison.

In the meantime, restless hands had moved on to the other wines. People had begun to open Freddie's wine and check its quality. Everyone approved. In addition, Doctor Sam placed an assortment of snacks across the large wooden table in his dining area. These snacks consisted of only the finest goods: imported sardines and anchovies, pickled mushrooms, pates, olives, smoked oysters, as well as many high quality smoked cheeses and sausages.

Disorderly consumption soon began to overtake everyone. I had brought eight bottles of wine, Freddie had brought seven, Jerry had brought along three and the others had brought varieties of beer. It became obvious that this evening was going to be a raucous one indeed. All of us but Jerry sat fully engrossed in consumption, swallowing, hacking and picking away at the food before us.

"Jerry," Doctor Sam told us, "was creating the best chili in Chippewa Harbor. In fact it's the best chili north of Detroit, maybe the best in the Universe my friends." At this time, Doctor Sam stood up, and pointed to Jerry, who was dipping his finger in the chili to judge the chili's current state of being. Doctor Sam clinked a fork on the side of his wine glass stating, "Gentlemen, gentlemen, do not distract the Chef!" We all bowed our heads and sat in silence for a brief moment. Jerry looked at all of us and professed things were progressing nicely.

As this was announced, the fellow sitting across from me whacked the table with his open hand and yelped out a loud cheer on Jerry's behalf. This loud bang and toast brought on more toasting, more laughter, more yelling and continued gorging. The increased trails of dribbled oil and crumbs and spilt beverages quickly took on the look of a nuclear meltdown.

A second round of cheers occurred shortly afterwards. Doctor Sam had left the table and soon after we heard a loud shout. Looking back we saw Doctor Sam with his eyes raised toward the heavens, as he declared, "My God fellas, it worked! We've got some brandy to taste!" To everyone's wide eyed pleasure, the first drops of pink elixir had been born.

Doctor Sam poured the contents of the flask into a small glass and passed it to those of us gathered at the table. Everyone in the group silently peered at the tiny dram. There before us sat the coveted liquid. This nectar was passed around and seemed to have been delivered straight from Cape Canaveral. It was potent. One of our group estimated it was well over one hundred proof. However, in addition to the strength, there was the secondary, rich fruit flavor of cherries. Jerry and Doctor Sam were quite pleased with the results. "We have discovered," proclaimed Doctor Sam, "our own private fountain of Kirsch!"

The quality of this elixir was pronounced by everyone to be superb! Of course this product, bolstered by the effects of the wine and beer already consumed, began to befuddle us all. An attempt was made by Jerry, while he simmered the chili, at serious conversation while the wine and Kirsch was passed around. Jerry tried to explain in his raspy, and now even more hoarse voice, what he felt were the drawbacks of the welfare system. Jerry tried to lead this discussion which in truth went nowhere but into argument and irrational bickering.

Freddie stated, as I remember it, "Listen Jerry, in this day and age most nations of industrial status provide some sort of safety net for their citizens. There are always those whose luck may have run out, or those who just can't keep a decent job."

Jerry, the blunt character that he was, became incensed at this comment. He flipped an angry face toward Freddie, spewing cigar ash into the chili, and shot back with strong indignation, large hands on his hips, "I ain't never been on the public dole. I've always been able ta support m'self!"

Doctor Sam, I noticed, was relishing this argument between two of his guests. He sat beaming in his large wooden chair while Jerry and Freddie bickered back and forth. After ten minutes or so, the weary, Kirsch heavy battlers became rather silent. Finally, Jerry pronounced that the chili was ready. Bowls were scooped full and I must admit, cigar ash and all, it was really quite good.

As we consumed the chili, everyone complemented Jerry on his culinary skills. At fairly frequent intervals, since the first magic drops of Kirsch had become available, Doctor Sam had been popping up to maintain the supply at the table. We were all becoming somewhat loopy, but still able to lacquer grand accolades upon the Kirsch. After three or four rounds of the flavored brandy, it was unanimous. The elixir was the best in the entire world!

The original plan by Doctor Sam was to bottle this product and place it in the far reaches of the refrigerator and then pass it out in small quantities, over many months. By the end of the party, though, there wasn't any left. This was perhaps the only goal which hadn't been accomplished by Doctor Sam and Jerry during this party. The evening had been a success. Great laughter had been shared along with camaraderie. The brief anger between Jerry and

Freddie had been smoothed over with the tastes and pleasures of the food and spirits.

Somewhere around midnight everyone slowly began to leave. As Freddie and I prepared to leave, we thanked both Doctor Sam and Jerry for a wonderful evening. We offered to assist them in cleaning up. The kitchen had taken on the appearance of a battlefield. Tin oyster containers were flung all about, wine bottles were lying everywhere, cheese was smeared on the tables, chili and Kirsch were sticking all about, as were sardines, bowls and plates. With smiles of gentlemanly aplomb, Doctor Sam said, "Oh no bother. Jerry and I will take care of things in the morning, but thanks for the offer."

Thus was my first experience with one of Doctor Sam and Jerry's legendary parties. By the time I moved from the area, both Doctor Sam and Jerry had remarried. Their mid-life suspicions of the female gender seemed to evaporate when they met the right women. Once married, Doctor Sam sold his somewhat remote lake home and resided full time in town. Although he occasionally ventured out to the water in the *Ruthie Lee*, he did so less and less frequently, grumbling that there were too many other boats on the water.

Jerry expanded his lumber operations into Wisconsin and began spending more and more of his time with his wife as well.

It wasn't long before these two friends started to drift apart. However, I believe they still cherish the time they spent together. Wherever these two may be today I can guarantee that fine wine, good food and an exceptional cigar are still part of their life-style. After all, these three elements can be essential to climbing the stairway to sublime happiness.

Another pair of buddies who left a lasting impression on me were a couple of older men from the fishing village of Dunbar. This pair of sidekicks were able to help and assist each other in a variety of useful ways. They were Bill Rilling and Ward Peterson. Bill was a retired Professor of Anthropology from Southern Michigan University who switched from being a long time summer resident, to full-time resident following his retirement. Ward was a native of the area and a very rare, if not the only, third generation commercial fisherman. He was known to everyone as Cap'n Ward. The life these two led was not one parallel with common society. They were a couple of living tangents who scratched their way into civilization from time to time. Their ability to remain positive as they lived a type of alternative life was what made them memorable to me.

Dunbar was a quiet little village along the coast of Lake Michigan, northwest of Chippewa Harbor. Bill was a distinguished looking gentleman with a flowing mane of long white hair and neatly clipped mustache. He carried himself quite straight and proper. He appeared aristocratic even in work clothes.

On the other hand, Cap'n Ward filled the perfect image of a weather beaten, sea faring individual. He was a casual and a bedraggled slump of a man, dressed in sloppy attire and a crooked captains cap, long sideburns streaming down the sides of his face. He always seemed to be shuffling along as best he could. The two had been friends years before Bill retired.

Perhaps they had first met because Bill owned some land on Little Bear Island off the coast of Dunbar. During his summer stays out on the island, it was Cap'n Ward who delivered supplies and mail, as well as bits of news from the outside world. At some point they befriended each other and then over the course of a few summers, built a summer cabin on the island. By the time I met these two, it seemed they both felt ownership of the island cabin.

The cabin itself demonstrated both Ward and Bill's skills as carpenters. Each of them were quite capable. Their lack of farsighted organization, however, did become obvious from time to time. The cabin was mostly stable and had survived year after year against all the forces of nature. There were details of amateur skill though. The joints creaked from time to time if more than one person stood in certain spots, the plumbing was mostly based on luck and one of the sleeping porches was so short that a person couldn't stand up. Yet, these were all little details it seemed to me, merely emphasizing the grand spirit of jerryrigging which made any stay at the cabin memorable and unique.

My wife and I were lucky to have several occasions to stay out at Bill and Ward's island cabin. Bill and I had some mutual friends from Southern Michigan University and, as well, Bill was friends with many of us in the Art Department.

Staying out on Little Bear Island was a truly glorious experience. The island had not yet been taken over by the National Park Service and there was only a small trickle of visitors. These grand visits to the island were full of solitude and the rich sounds of island life. The crash of the waves, the flight of gulls, the filtering of sunlight through trees during the day and grand swimming. Bill's cabin was only about fifty yards from the waterfront which made it easy to wander and explore the land.

When exploring the gray, abandoned homes and sheds that still stood on the island, I often caught myself imagining what life might have been like for those few farmers who once lived on the here. This island getaway was, from morning to night, like a dreamland. It was easy to sit on the porch at night with a generous tumbler of finely aged bourbon and become carried off with the whistle of a faraway lake steamer, the caress of waves on the sand, a full moon, or the gentle breezes across the land.

Somehow Bill and Ward had carted a rusty old jeep to the island. This lump of iron and steel was capable of being used from time to time if good fortune and the ignition system were on your side. Granted, a tetanus shot seemed in order prior to sitting on the exposed and rusty springs sticking out of the seats, but once the jeep was running, it did prove to be an interesting way to move around the island, using the old farming roads.

However, as summers went by, Bill knew that things were destined to change. He had been following the intentions of the National Park Service and understood they intended to purchase the island and create what was to become the National Western Michigan Lake Shore Park. This motivated Bill to purchase a building lot in the town of Dunbar itself three or four years prior to his eviction off Little Bear Island. About two years before his retirement from the island, he and Ward began the construction of a new house.

Bill was not known for following standard procedures. When he placed the stakes for his new home in Dunbar he did so with a sense of rough estimation. When he showed Cap'n Ward his plans, Ward cautiously asked, "Now Bill, did you have this properly surveyed first?"

Bill responded, "Well, yes, I remember a marker stone being right about here and so I've come back about ten feet. Wouldn't want to invade on anyone else."

The basement was then dug and cement poured. The frame itself was prepared by outside help. Once this was done, Bill and Ward intended to finish the house on their own. The only hitch that occurred was when Bill's neighbor arrived for the summer and stared at the framed shell which seemed a little too close. When his neighbor looked into the matter, it became apparent that Bill had placed a good slice of his basement in his neighbor's yard. This was typical for Bill, who continually ignored the good advice of his friend Cap'n Ward. Bills efforts at avoiding expenses and cutting corners almost always led to a thousand pains and more expenses later on. Fortunately, Bill had developed a knack for digging himself out of troubles such as this and construction on the house continued as planned.

When Bill and Ward worked together, conversation could escalate and differences shouted out for hours. Over the course of a day though they always managed to twist and iron things out. In fact the two of them were normally seen together at the Galloping Goose Cafe in high spirits, shedding their thirsts with beer, chuckling over poorly sawn boards and hammers which had fallen on each others heads. It slowly became apparent why these two were friends. It would have been hard for anyone else to work closely with either of them.

Both had been married for a time, but each had been divorced as well. Probably to avoid lonesomeness, they stuck together. This was no small task. Even Bill's dog, Chester, took a disliking to Bill.

The local story was that one evening, after perhaps a little too much to drink at the Goose, Bill returned to his car with Chester and on the way home, feel asleep at the wheel. At which point he went straight off the road, on to the Dunbar golf course, only to ram into a tree near the fairway. Chester and Bill were unharmed, yet that was the last time anyone ever saw the dog travel with Bill again.

To most people, and especially the older residents in Dunbar, these two were considered hazards, even dangerous. Whether it was building houses, or chopping wood these two always seemed to inflict a bit of trouble on others. They were in fact considered a wrecking crew by one table of older men who gathered in the corner each morning at the Galloping Goose.

There were countless tales of their rather oblivious antics around Dunbar. One day in the late fall they were removing Bill's sailboat from Lake Michigan when the trailer blew a tire in the middle of the road. As the tire went flat, the boat slipped off the trailer and slid to the ground. To fix this problem Bill and Ward jacked the trailer up, removed the flat tire and drove off, leaving the boat and the trailer in the busy street with no explanation, or even a note of what was going on. Instead, they took the flat tire to a local filling station, and then, when informed that the repair would take about an hour, these two adventurers decided to go to the Goose, consume a couple mugs of cold beer and wait. Well, a couple mugs of beer led to a few more mugs and soon it had been four or five hours. The two of them leisurely strolled out into the blaring summer sun, picked up the repaired tire and returned to a small and frustrated group of confused tourists and irritated residents. During the last few hours people had been forced to slowly eek around the sailboat and trailer. Without apology, or explanation, Bill and Ward, with the assistance of some onlookers, replaced the missing tire, returned the boat to the trailer and drove the five blocks back to Bill's house.

This wasn't the end of the day for Bill and Ward though. Bill still intended to store his boat for the coming winter and had decided that a good place for this would be amongst a small grove of birch trees next to his driveway. Unfortunately, while backing the boat in amongst the trees his boat trailer became tightly wedged between two birch trees. No matter how much gas was punched through the engine the trailer wouldn't budge. The two men sat for a moment in silence. Bill turned to Ward and said, "Listen, I have an idea. I'll climb on the stern of the boat and brace my feet on the left and push forward on the tree to the right. When I give the signal, drive forward."

Bill then climbed upon the boat and began to push the birch tree away from the boat. He then shouted, "Okay, Ward, pull 'er out!"

When Ward gunned the engine, the trailer did lurch forward, but a tree limb, which had been bent backward, flung forward and whacked Bill on the side of his head. Ward slammed on the brakes and ran back. Bill had fallen to the ground and was laying unconscious in a heap, surrounded by birch leaves. Ward became extremely nervous, picked Bill up and carried him inside in hopes of revival.

Ward laid Bill on a couch, grabbed a pot of cold water and tossed it across Bill's face. At first nothing happened. In fact Bill's normally crimson colored face had even begun to turn blue. Ward placed a blanket over Bill, blotted the blood off his face and applied more cold water with a towel. Slowly, Bill recovered consciousness, and staggered to his elbows. Grimacing in pain, he asked, "Ward, what the hell happened?"

Ward answered, "Bill, one of the birch trees snapped forward like a rubber band and hit you right in the side of the head. God, I thought you were a goner!" Ward then added, "Bill, geez, do you have anything in the house to drink?"

At which time Bill, still nursing his tender head, replied, "Well, yes I do Ward, but I don't feel much like a drink right now."

To which Ward responded, "No, Bill, not for you, my God, not for you, for me. This has been one of the most terrible experiences of my whole life!"

By now these two are quite old men and in the declining years of their lives. Neither is able to venture too far from their homes. Each has family members who live nearby and who assist them in daily chores. Yet, they are not forgotten. If one were to walk into the Galloping Goose and mention their names, people would still have a good time rehashing the exploits of these two very close friends.

Chapter Sixteen
Rural Recluses

The person choosing to be alone, the recluse, seems to be more obvious in the country than in a city. I remember my first glimpse of this style of life and the curiosity it inspired. I was in the back seat of a car with my parents on some country road when I spotted a rusty, beat up trailer in a corner of a wood lot. I'd asked my mother what the trailer was doing there and her reply was, "Oh, I think an old Indian woman lives there." We must have been near my hometown in east central Michigan, or else how would my mother have known that? As the years of my youth passed, whenever encountering an old trailer, or rusting school bus tucked away in the woods, I would wonder who lived there. I was curious why someone would want to live away from rivers, or towns, or lakes, apart from other people and activities. Were these people scared? Had they been run out of town? It was hard for me to comprehend that anyone might be comfortable hidden from view and left alone.

As I began in earnest to work toward higher degrees of learning, attempting to build a career, hopefully as an artist and teacher, I stopped noticing as I did when a child, the lone country hermit. Even when I lived for a period of time in Appalachia I was just too busy to notice. My interests and attentions were directed elsewhere.

This changed when I became accustomed to my surroundings in Chippewa Harbor. I rediscovered my childhood fascination with the recluse. Shortly after we were married, Liz and I befriended two artists living near Fredericksburg, about thirty miles southwest of Chippewa Harbor. The first time we drove down there we passed through the village of Paradise. Outside of this little village I spotted a small, strange looking house covered with faded, green tar paper. It sat forlornly at the edge of a twenty

194

acre field. No trees or shrubs were nearby to provide shade or wind protection. In fact I could see no sign of any attempts to keep up the yard or house. Tall, wild field grasses seemed to have grown into the front door.

I said nothing about this house to my friends that day. Rather, during the following week, while at work, I asked Russell Vanderbeck about this lonely dwelling. I remembered that Russell had grown up near Fredericksburg and might know something. At this time Russell was a student of mine. I asked him while we were outside, behind the fine arts building, taking our traditional midday smoke break. Immediately after I made my inquiry, Russell responded, "Oh, I know which place you mean. That little place belongs to Indian Jake. He's been around for a long time. I think he's on welfare, disability, or something. I gave him a ride home once. He talked a lot, but I couldn't understand much he said."

Russell went on to say that sometimes, in early November, the Sheriff would drive out to Jake's and announce, "Jake, get some extra clothes together and your toothbrush. I'm arresting you for vagrancy this winter. They say it's gonna be a bad one." Jake would happily comply with the Sheriff's request as the prospect of three meals a day and a warm bed until spring sounded quite appealing. Jake was always content to spend the winter reading magazines, taking baths and generally being cared for in jail.

This was one way for some of the townspeople to watch over Jake during hard times.

Several months passed, perhaps even a year, before I had my first sighting of Jake. I knew it must be him, even glimpsed from a distance. While I was driving down into the village of Paradise I noticed a hunched figure making his way slowly uphill toward me. Limited northbound traffic had taken away the opportunity for him to hitchhike, so Jake was slowly trudging home on foot. As I went by I noticed he was wearing a heavy plaid, flannel shirt. Green, baggy, work pants which stopped an inch or two above his ankles and a pair of well-traveled boots. He appeared to be bowlegged, perhaps from rickets. His face was brown and wrinkled. Unruly black and gray hair blew every which way in the breeze. His head was bowed down as he moved, either because he had to concentrate on where he stepped, or out of humility, probably both.

During the many years that we lived in northern Michigan and the many occasions that I drove to Fredericksburg, I saw Jake only one more time. This time he was walking downhill into Paradise for some meager supplies, I imagined. The weather was quite warm, yet I observed that he was wearing his flannel shirt again and the same baggy trousers. The downhill walk seemed to require less effort. He stood a bit more upright as he moved, but his bowed legs still seemed unsteady. My curiosity was rekindled as to how he, or any other hermit spends his solitary hours. Did he have a television? A radio? Did he read old magazines, or just sleep? As if a child again, I was captivated and confused regarding the life-style of the recluse.

Jake is gone now, but I understand that a Native American family, perhaps relatives of his, own the property and have built a home of their own at the southwest corner of the open field. Jake's little green, tar paper house is still standing though, perhaps being left as a silent and windswept tribute in his memory.

About the same time Jake was revealed to me, I discovered another interesting man of solitary habits. One evening Liz and I had accepted a dinner invitation from Matt McDaniel, a local artist, and his wife, Katy. They had recently purchased a little farm and were in the process of upgrading their new house and what I still consider the smallest barn I've ever seen. The place was nestled in a wooded area about eight miles southwest of Fredericksburg, on a back road. As we entered the house we were both pleased with the aromas good food. Katy informed all of us it would be at least another half hour until dinner was ready and so we were to make ourselves at home. While waiting and making small talk, Matt walked us around the house, allowing us to admire his still life paintings. A couple were winter landscapes, which Matt referred to as his, "white on white specials." Hanging alone on a narrow dining room wall was the portrait of a gentle looking little man with raggedy gray hair, a stubby beard and twinkling blue eyes. He was dressed in a rumpled, gray, tweed jacket matched with a blue work shirt buttoned all the way up. I asked, "Matt, who is this interesting fellow?"

Matt replied, "Oh, that's old Gus Bauer. You passed his cedar shaked home a mile east of here. We had to bribe him with four Sunday dinners before I could get him to agree to sit for me." Matt was evidently quite pleased we had noticed this painting.

Katy heard my question from the kitchen as well and seconded Matt's appreciation for this man. After we were all seated for dinner, both Matt and Katy tried to piece together the saga of Gustav Bauer.

It seems as if his parents were immigrants from Germany who had landed in the late 1870's at the bustling Lake Michigan port town of Fredericksburg. Upon arrival, the Bauers left Fredericksburg, trudging eastward along the Herring River until Mr. Bauer saw a spring up on a hillside. It was near this spring that the Bauers decided to build their first house, anxious to start a family and a new life in this wild new world.

At first the family lived in a sod house while Mr. Bauer cleared the land so he could establish his life in farming. Soon his first son, Gustav, was born. It wasn't clear what year this had been since no birth certificate had been filed. Gustav himself could no longer remember what he had been told was his birthday. It was guessed to be about 1888. Four other children were born, two sisters and two brothers. Other than a sister, who was married in Fredericksburg, the whereabouts of the rest of Gus' siblings was unclear to him.

Perhaps around 1890, Mr. Bauer was able to afford a more suitable wooden framed house. A barn and other outbuildings followed. This second house was the very one Gustav now lived in. It was built in a National Folk Style, similar to the house which Liz and I owned, but Gus' was sided with cedar shakes. Cedar shake roofs were common in the late 19th century, but the Bauer house was the only one I'd seen with cedar shakes used as siding in the area. The two story house had living and sleeping areas placed in the middle, a kitchen and dining area built in a wing off the side.

When Matt and Katy bought their little farm in 1968, the Arvidson's, a neighbor couple, came by to welcome them to the area. During the ensuing conversation, Matt inquired if anyone lived in the old farm down the road. Mrs. Arvidson replied, "Oh, yes, old Gus Bauer lives there." Then, almost apologetically, she continued, "but it didn't always look like that. When Gus' mother was alive you can bet she kept things right." She went on to explain how the lawn had always been mowed, the shrubs well trimmed, the curtains washed, flower and vegetable gardens carefully tended to. She added that Gus was a nice man though, even if he didn't mow the lawn. She encouraged Matt and Katy to introduce themselves as Gus was a bit shy about that sort of thing.

Before they knew of Gustav, Matt and Katy had examined the tattered property where Gus lived. It never crossed their minds that someone may still live on the premises. After all, the house sat looming, in weather beaten fashion—the front porch half sealed off by a lilac bush. Poplar trees and several rose vines had gone berserk and looked entwined with the cedar shakes. The remains of a once well tended flower garden, bordered with scattered rocks, was now all but obliterated by tall grass. From the screenless windows, opened for ventilation, fluttered the tattered remnants of Mrs. Bauer's once-proud curtains. Curtains which were now more like ghosts dancing in the wind. When Matt saw cattle behind the weathered barn, he thought for sure that the place was being rented for pasture by another farmer and that the house was empty. The whole vision of dilapidation was made complete by a dented and rusty, blue faded 1952 Chevy truck parked askew in the front yard. It seemed to be half buried in weeds and grass.

One day, during his first summer at his new house, Matt was driving into town when he noticed that the county had mowed the tall grass by the side of the road. On his return home, he saw, out beside the road, an old man and the previously half buried, faded blue pickup idling with a light trail of exhaust coming out. There stood an old man loading the cut grass with a pitch fork on to the rear of the truck so that he could feed it to his cattle. This sight was quite a surprise for Matt since he was certain the place had been vacant. Shortly thereafter, he and Katy decided they did need to take Mrs. Arvidson's advice and pay a visit to their strange, old neighbor, which they did, the following Sunday afternoon.

Matt and Katy turned into the lane leading up to Gus' weather beaten home and parked beside the blue pickup. As they neared the front porch the aging screen door squeaked and a gentle looking old man emerged, dressed in dusty bib overalls and a frayed denim jacket. "Hello, Mr. Bauer," Katy said, "I'm Katy McDaniel and this is my husband, Matt. We just moved into the old Kramer place and we just wanted to stop by and introduce ourselves."

Gus smiled and rather quickly said, "I'm glad you stopped by." Then he sat down in a weathered wooden rocker, bidding his guests to sit on the steps. He was obviously quiet and shy, but still eager to meet his new neighbors. He suddenly appeared less of a hermit than a genuine country eccentric.

This brief introduction led to more visits. Eventually Matt and Katy started having Gus over for an occasional Sunday dinner. As the friendship grew, more of Gus' unconventional life-style unfolded through comments by neighbors and conversations with Gus himself.

It turned out that his mother had died about fifteen years ago. When Matt first entered the Bauer home it was rather obvious that regular housekeeping hadn't been practiced since Gus' mother deceased. Aside from the ragged curtains, there were worn area rugs, encapsulated by dust and debris. The furniture, except for Gus' favorite reading chair, had all been pushed to the edges of the rooms and heaped with clothing, hand tools and newspapers. Apparently Gus subscribed to one of the daily Detroit newspapers and read it each evening. There was a small table and lamp beside his chair for this purpose.

The farming operation as directed by Gus was equally haphazard. In his younger days, with his father, he had planted corn on land across the road for animal feed, but that land had since been sold. Since then the pigs and the chickens had simply vanished as far as Gus could remember. He did, however, still carefully tend to six dairy cows. He called them his pets. Not only did he carefully gather the roadside grass when it was so conveniently cut by the county, but he scavenged old bread and wilted vegetables from behind the supermarket in town. The sandy and hilly land wasn't really fertile enough to be dependable pasture.

One day when Matt arrived to visit with Gus, he was asked if he might be able to help mend some fence line. It happened that once again Gus' pets had gotten out and made a beeline for the Arvidson's orchard where there was plenty of lush vegetation.

In the process of enjoying a rare banquet, Gus' pets had trampled and damaged some irrigation hoses as well. Mr. Arvidson was not too happy with any of this. As Matt walked along the fence with Gus he noticed that the fence consisted of a few strands of sagging wire and wobbly posts. The trouble spot, however, was an area where old bedsprings and discarded wooden shipping palettes had been wired together to form a makeshift fence. During a wind storm, or just by age, this haphazard section had fallen apart. Gus remarked, as they once again collaged the palettes and bed springs together, "There's a lot o' good wire in these things. Shame that people throw 'em away like they do."

Gus made trips to town not only to gather discarded produce for his beloved cattle, but sometimes he would venture in for personal business. Occasionally he would frequent the barber shop, or need to have his wonder truck worked on by Kenny Miles, the kindhearted mechanic whose wizardry kept the fading blue truck alive. On some trips in to town Gus would inexplicably "dress up." Ordinarily this wouldn't have been a problem except that Gus stored his good clothes on a pulley in his dairy barn where they accumulated rather acrid odors which would drift off when he walked around town, causing people to snicker and roll their eyes behind his back.

As the years passed by, neighbors began to notice that Gus was losing his ability to care for the farm as well as himself. Although not always pleased with Gus, the Arvidsons remained the classic, good neighbors once associated with the rural American life-style. Mrs. Arvidson began to take one hot meal a day to Gus. Mr. Arvidson instructed his sons to cut firewood for the old man as winter approached. When Gus' well pump burnt out, the sons began to carry water for him. As the Arvidson's became regular visitors inside the house, they noticed that Gus had begun to simply live in his kitchen, having dragged a brass bed in by the wood stove. For more heat, Gus left the stove door open at night and the old kitchen was soon gaining a patina of soot. That's when the Arvidson's convinced Gus to sell his remaining cattle. It was obvious that he was too feeble to care for them.

On what was thought to be Gus' eighty-eighth birthday, the McDaniel's had him over for dinner. His bright blue eyes sparked with joy. He was very appreciative and spent hours talking until Matt and Katy had to insist that he be taken home.

It wasn't long after this happy birthday event that all the neighbors became convinced Gus had to leave the old farm home for his own safety. They urged Katy McDaniel to call the county social worker to pay a visit on Gus in order to convince him he'd be better off in the local nursing home. Much to everyone's surprise, Gus readily agreed. The court appointed him a guardian and the chores of his estate and farm were taken care of.

Gus was taken to the county nursing home and thrived on the steady flow of food and the luxury of a regular bath, something which had not been possible in his own home, at least since the demise of his well. Not only was he declared to have lived one hundred years, but his good nature and sparkling appreciation of others charmed the nursing staff until his death. As Matt McDaniel often said, "Gus is far too gentle for the world around him."

Another situation involving rural isolation was the story of John Nurley's family, who once owned a prosperous farm southwest of Stanleyville and directly west of the classic old farmstead which had been purchased by Luther Runquist.

Luther had given several of us a booklet published by the county 4-H program which detailed Tamarack County, identifying each farm and its owner. This booklet was quite useful to me as I was always on the look out for obscure places which I could use for landscape drawings, or photographs.

One morning during late August I decided to examine a spot I noticed in Luther's little 4-H booklet. I remember it was a cool and quiet morning. Soft round clouds had slowly developed, carrying a hint of autumn. I told Liz of my plan, but she declined to accompany me as she didn't normally share my enthusiasm for exploring forlorn and unsafe structures on abandoned farms, nor was she as affected as I was by the romantic nostalgia that often overwhelmed me at such places. She only insisted that I wear my heavy work shoes as a protection against rusty nails and wire.

My first stop was Luther Runquist's deserted collection of derelict buildings including the remains of the grand, old Victorian home. From there I selected the road I was curious about exploring. About six or seven miles from Luther's I noticed, on my right side, a tight cluster of farm buildings through a thicket of overgrown trees. I slowed down to a crawl to better examine what I had found. I decided to enter this area and inched into the old remains of a driveway. The old farm house was in rather sad condition and the porch, like Gus Bauer's, was almost obliterated by a grove of poplar saplings and untamed grass. I had, indeed, discovered a real classic. I was overcome with excitement.

I drove on in, parked behind the house and emerged from the car to survey the scene before me. Ahead of me was a grand, weathered barn which still stood proud and strong. The house on the other hand was near ruination. There were four other sheds of varied sizes still standing true. Stacked in the rafters of two of the sheds were planks and boards of different lengths and widths consisting of local hardwoods such as walnut, oak and maple. Obviously milled locally as the rough saw grooves were clearly evident. I was tempted to rummage through them and perhaps take some home with me, but when I considered taking the wood, I seemed to feel some phantom guard watching over me. I decided to leave the wood planks alone. There really felt to be a pall of desperation and sadness all around me.

Walking behind the large barn I discovered a 1920's corn harvester rotting in the growth of tall weeds. Beside this piece of equipment rested two rusty, horse drawn hay rakes and a four bottomed plow, all parked in a neat row. To the left of all these old farm utensils appeared to be the remains of a cedar shake planing mill, though most of the machinery and belts which would have been required for planing were gone. To the north was a field of maybe fifty to sixty acres that had been planted in navy beans. Obviously someone leased the land for crops. I severely doubted if anyone was living in the main house. It looked too far gone, much more than even Gustav Bauer's home.

My curiosity to investigate the main house was burning me up. So off I went. The back entrance went through an outdoor pantry area, which must have been added in later years. The main body of the house dated from around the turn of the century, but certainly didn't possess the detailed grandeur of Luther's crumbling old country palace. The rear door inside the pantry, which led into the house, had long since fallen off its hinges and now lay across the floor like a weathering corpse. To the immediate right of the back door and pantry area was a windmill and a water tank which would have supplied a luxurious gravity fed water system to the kitchen. I thought, as I stood in the pantry area, that this place must have been quite prosperous and well managed during its time. Reaching my hand out to grasp the doorknob I noticed that the wind picked up and the windmill began to creak. I looked over again and saw that there was an upside down star painted on the windmill fin and that the fan blades had begun to slowly creak around.

After a slow walk through the downstairs, I undertook to investigate the upper floor. Between the dining room and the living room, a dark and narrow stairway led up to the bedrooms. I carefully made my way up the creaking, loose stairs. When I reached the top step I was unprepared for the sight before me. There were four bedrooms and each was completely piled, at least waist high, wall to wall, with stacks of old papers and magazines such as *Farmer's Almanacs*, *Saturday Evening Post's*, *Colliers* and *Popular Mechanics*. Nothing had been discarded.

I cautiously opened the back door and entered what was the kitchen. The interior of the house was bare except for a metal sink in the kitchen. Tattered curtains adorned the window frames. All the varnish in the house had become dry and checked. The bare plank floors were dust covered and worn looking. Gaudy flowered wallpaper was sagging and slipping from its moorings. The house had an abandoned odor of dirt, mold and mice, of which I was somewhat fond of, associating with surprise and mystery.

All the covers were designed in pre-WW II styles. This vast plateau of old paper was sprinkled as well with chunks of fallen plaster and cobwebs. I examined a closet and found more of the same, boxes of toilet paper roll cores, spools of twine, old containers of soap, shoe laces, ribbons, bows, paper clips. I heard the whine of bees and noticed that a hive had taken up residence inside the ceiling of one of the bedroom closets.

Within a few minutes, I began to feel uncomfortable and spooked. This house felt rather morbid to me. It still felt occupied by its old owners. I was convinced that its former inhabitants had lived in an atmosphere of unhappiness and desperation, perhaps in social isolation and sadness. As I made my way back down the crumbling stairs I spotted a notebook atop a pile of old magazines. I blew away the dust and discovered that it was a diary. In faded ink was an inscription on the cover, "Private Property of Inez Hurley." I picked this notebook up and retreated down the stairs as if I were a lucky archeologist. I proceeded back outside and felt very relieved. I took a seat on the back step of the house and began to peer at the notebook's contents.

The first few pages of the diary randomly described daily life and the workings of the farm. I cannot remember the exact dates the diary began, but I do remember it was the autumn of either 1923, or 24. As the diary entered the winter months, the writing took on the feeling of loneliness and depression. There were also many pages of poetry. The writing seemed too sophisticated, somehow too familiar, to have been written by a young farm girl. As I continued to scan through the diary, I was soon blown away.

The beginning of one page toward the end of the diary opened with, "I told mother that I wanted to move to Chippewa Harbor today and get a job. I need a life away from here, but mother said, 'No.' She was very upset and angrily warned me that the Devil was waiting in Chippewa Harbor. The town was a Sodom and Gemorrah. She absolutely forbade me to go." This was enough. I hastily put the diary down and tossed it, along with my camera and drawing pencils into the car and left. It felt as if I was being watched again.

When the college began classes again during September I walked over to the Admissions Office to visit with Bill Watson, an admission's counselor. I knew that at one time Bill had been an employee of the county sheriff's department and that he might have some knowledge on the nature of my discovery. While I breathlessly described the old farm and the diary, Bill cut in and said, starting with a deep sigh, "Oh, boy, Jack, do I ever know exactly where you were. The old Hurley farm. Geez, they were REALLY something out there."

Bill went on to relate that this area, out by Stanleyville, had once been a hotbed of old time Christian Fundamentalism. The Hurley sisters,

Martha and Inez, had been ruled by the iron fists of their parents. The daughters were instructed not to ever speak to any other children at the county schoolhouse. They were only allowed to speak with other children who attended their church on Sunday. The daughters were never allowed an excursion to Chippewa Harbor which, in those days, had a population of around five to six thousand people. The daughters were only allowed a few hurried shopping trips into Stanleyville. I also discovered, from Bill, that the poetry I had read in the diary was most likely copied from books which the family had mail ordered. It turns out the postman was the only real contact the daughters had with the outside world they had so badly wanted to explore as children.

Bill went on to tell of John Hurley's later years. One day, after finishing an Autumn corn harvest, John had neatly parked his machinery out behind his barn and declared that the farming business was too hard. He would never farm again. Aside from caring for his cattle, he never did do any more field work. Bill estimated that this occurred when Mr. Hurley was about eighty years old.

A few years after old John stopped working, a distant cousin from Stanleyville stopped in to check on the Hurleys. Aside from the neighbor who had begun to work the land, this cousin was one of the few visitors who ever saw the Hurleys. The local church had been disbanded, so there were only a few friends remaining from the Hurleys fundamentalist flock, leaving them quite alone. As this cousin entered the living area, he was suddenly jolted by the sight of John Hurley slumped over, dead, on a Victorian love seat. When the daughters were asked why they didn't notice this, Martha replied, with a glassy, distant stare, "Oh, we wondered why Papa stopped arguing with the Bible yesterday." By this time Mrs. Hurley was deceased as well, leaving the daughters, now in the later years of their own lives, alone in the house.

I sat in Bill's office with my mouth open, in total amazement, hardly able to believe the saga he was revealing. Bill wasn't finished though. He continued telling me how, after their father died, the two sisters became even more eccentric. In fact, within months, the farmer who was renting the Hurleys land complained to the sheriff that the animals were being badly neglected. Upon inspection, the animals were removed and auctioned off. When the Sheriff's deputy scolded the sisters for their neglect, Inez, wearing the same blank stare that her sister had used when responding to their dead father, nodded her head slowly and repeated over and over, "The Lord will provide. You'll see, the Lord will provide." She seemed to be speaking to some imaginary person, as if hypnotized.

As the years continued, passersby at night would occasionally see lanterns shining in the woods while the sisters gathered plants and roots, such as brackenferns, under moonlight. Even before their father had passed on, the sisters had moved downstairs, since the upper rooms had become too filled with their strange and hoarded treasures. They were occasionally seen tending a small garden and some of the fruit trees, but it was not clear to Bill who tended to their other needs, or how often.

In any case, when the sisters were well into their seventies, the sheriff was called in again. A neighbor had found the two sisters suffering from starvation. When asked why they hadn't opened any of the many fruit and vegetables canned in the cellar, Inez, answered, staring vacantly as before, "Oh, Sheriff, Mama always told us to put aside something for a rainy day." The poor sisters didn't realize how hard it was raining.

Bill went on to explain that the sisters were taken to a nursing home weak, malnourished and confused. The local bank took over the estate. An auction was held. Rumor had it that the banker from Stanleyville and his wife stole the good china and the more valuable antique furniture prior to the auction. Bill seemed to think this had all happened around 1962. Since it was now 1975, he was certain the sisters were deceased.

Suddenly there was a knock at the door. A student was waiting to speak with Bill. I mumbled my appreciation to Bill for his enlightening tale and stumbled back to my office in a daze.

My friend in the English department, Bandy McPherson, also enjoyed rides in the open country from time to time. He relished taking photographs of the rich landscape, as well as deserted farm yards. We had made several countryside trips together, each questing after the subtle images where shadows might dance and blend with old apple trees, or across weathered barn doors.

The next time I saw Bandy, I eagerly told him what I had found out about the Hurley farm. I guaranteed him a day of photo opportunities. We picked a day when neither of us had any classes to teach and declared it was essential that we get out of town for an afternoon of Research and Development! On the day we had agreed upon, we left for the Hurley place with a cooler full of beer and sandwiches. Our cameras were loaded with film.

Upon our arrival, Bandy and I spent a lot of time taking photographs of the sheds, textured barnwood, neatly organized farm equipment and the sagging windmill. After a couple hours I urged Bandy to follow me inside the house and up the stairs, where, I promised, lay a clutter of items that would be great material for a short story. Upon gazing at the mountains of magazines, the fallen plaster and weird contents of the closets, Bandy, not normally queasy at the sight of despair, declared, "Jack, I can't stay here any longer. This place is unholy or something. I have to leave." The closet full of toilet paper cores seemed to have befuddled and struck some sort of fear in Bandy. Something about the strange and oppressed minds that had lived here still remained a strong influence. We both knew that these piles of saved items were in relation to some nebulous usage, certainly they weren't being saved as fire starters.

Bandy was sitting outside drinking a beer by the time I finished taking a couple more photos. On my way back to the car I spied down into the basement cellar and even spotted the aging mason jars on the shelves, the ones full of beans and peas being saved for a "rainy day."

Our early departure from the Hurley place was all right with me since I had already taken an ample number of photos. We still had the shank of the day ahead of us though, so I pulled out Luther Runquist's 4-H booklet and found a nearby road which we agreed to take, in search of more material to photograph and explore.

After driving a couple of miles down a road lined with old maple trees, I spotted another interesting, abandoned treasure trove of buildings beneath the shade of large and looming trees.

I swung into the unused driveway and parked the car near the main house. As we entered the door to this house, there was a faded, stamped metal sign above us which read, "Jesus Saves." The kitchen cupboards were made of some sort of dark 1940's paneling. The curtains in the living room were a dark and bloody maroon with ugly flowers printed on them. Very little light was being allowed in. A few dark, overstuffed chairs and a brooding couch were being kept company by two cheap end tables. As I proceeded further, in search of a stairway, I heard a strong wind pick up outside and a series of creaks and even felt the movement of the house floor. I looked back and Bandy's eyes had become wide open with terror. He quickly became nervous again and declared, "Sorry Jack, I gotta get outa here. This place, this whole area is giving me the willy's. I NEVER want to come back here."

On our way back to the car, I managed, while stumbling through the thick weeds, to snap a couple of dramatic photos of a fallen barn. We then made a hasty departure. On the way home, Bandy insisted that I take the long way back to avoid seeing the Hurley place again. I can't remember if the photos I took of this last house turned out or not.

Perhaps I made two more trips back to the Hurley house. Finally I couldn't go back anymore either. I did give the diary I had found on my first trip to a writer friend of mine who wanted to create a short story around it, but I have no idea whether she ever did or not. As far as I know this may be the only written record of this tragic family.

CHAPTER SEVENTEEN
PARADE PRANKSTERS

T he history of human civilization is often times a long series of mundane chores, suddenly accented with festivals and celebrations. I've found the public festival to be of great importance on the influence of local life. A force that gives society, a region, and the people shape and purpose since festivals vary according to climates, seasons, locale and ethnic backgrounds. It is common to rejoice in the arrival of spring, or to praise the glory of a bountiful fall harvest. It is known that many pagan societies held some form of festive event to honor and worship various gods and goddesses in an effort to win spiritual favor. We have absorbed the festival in our time as well.

In my life time, especially after World War II, I've witnessed the festival go through a continued evolution. When I was very young, I was aware of tiny, local festivals. The type that celebrate the founding of a town, that paid tribute to the ethnic populations of the area, or which drew attention to the particular agricultural speciality of an area. As time has gone on, these little publicized, regional festivals have been given new looks by more aggressive Chamber of Commerce committees seeking to bring more money into town and strengthen the local business climate. It's become apparent that new Gods have come into play as chamber members attempt to sway the spirits of capital gains. This type of cash oriented worship has altered the scope of older festivals, harming the local and authentic flavor, as well as the original meanings intended by local communities.

When investigating the number of various festivals around the country, the results can be staggering. One discovers Crab Festivals, Chili Festivals, Sweet Corn Fests, Broom Corn, Apple, Peaches, Peas ... all sorts of celebrations. Well, the state of Michigan is no different. The state hosts a wide variety of festivals from asparagus and Bavarian beer fests, to navy beans and morel mushrooms. In Chippewa Harbor the local fruit growers celebrated the cherry. This festival has slowly grown to be one of the largest celebrations in the state.

The Fruit Growers' Cherry Fest was originally organized in the mid-1920's as a sort of ritual to celebrate the end of the cherry harvest. This celebration really began in the spring when local clergymen would perform the Blessing of the Blossoms. This was a prayer and plea to God for abundant fruit, no late frosts and a good market price. In July, when the sweet cherries were picked, the festival was held to celebrate the end of the season and hard work. The celebration included a small parade of local dignitaries, a squad of World War I veterans and usually a float or two sponsored by the larger businesses in town. The audience was mostly locals as tourism was in its fledgling state. Working people, farmers, the long-term summer residents and a smattering of folks from surrounding villages lined the streets to watch and mark the end of another growing season. Then, after the "serious" parade, the locals were given the opportunity for their own Mummers Parade. This was a light hearted spoof on the serious town parade. Farmers, many from North Bay township, would decorate their horses and wagons with ribbons, a steam tractor might chug down the street festooned with weed flowers and someone would normally feature their outhouse on a flatbed trailer. The atmosphere was generally one of clowning around and letting off the stress following the truly back braking work involved in old fashioned fruit picking. The Mummers Parade was banned after a few years for reasons I was never able to discern. Perhaps the rural people became too rowdy for the genteel townspeople. Unfortunately the Mummers Parade ended years before I arrived. It was only kept alive by the dim and diminishing memories of the older folks I encountered.

As luck would have it, during my first summer in town, while living at Abe's rickety apartment, the route for the Fruit Grower's Parade passed only two blocks away.

It was Friday evening during the festival while I was outside enjoying a smoke on my little upstairs porch when Abe pulled into his parking spot. I hollered down to him, "Hey, Abe! What time does the parade start tomorrow?"

He quickly replied, "Oh, about 10 o'clock and passes the corner by Danny's Bar & Grill at a quarter to eleven. Ya wanna watch it together?"

I said that I would and asked how early we must leave to get ourselves a good vantage point.

His instant reply was, "Aw, we won't wanna stand on the street. Let me talk to Danny. I'll get back to you. A damn festival anyway! I had to detour all the way south just to get home. Christ, there's tourists everywhere."

This was the first time I had heard a local citizen criticize the festival. I had assumed it was an event everyone looked forward to. I soon learned that the unenthusiastic viewpoint held by Abe was shared by many others.

Danny's Bar & Grill was a neighborhood bar and local institution similar to Sladek's, but without the historical mystique, or colorful interior I enjoyed. It was, however, located in what used to be an old and rather important business district on the west side of Chippewa Harbor. Unfortunately, much of the historical appearance of this district had been ruined by rather tasteless remodeling. Thankfully, Danny's exterior was untouched, although the interior had been remodeled and was quite stark. It was lined with artificial wood paneling.

Later in the evening I heard the excited charge of Abe up the stairs to my apartment. I opened the door and Abe was beaming. He had obtained permission from Danny to watch the parade from the second floor storage area of the Bar & Grill. Abe was proud of this achievement because it set us apart from the common tourist on the street who had to set up camp by eight a.m. for a good spot. We, on the other hand, could waltz in at a leisurely, somewhat gentlemanly time. We agreed to meet at a quarter after ten.

Saturday morning dawned crisp and bright, unusually cool for the second week in July. I met Abe out front of the apartment and we walked the couple blocks to the corner where Danny's stood. As we approached, the throng of onlookers loomed before us. There were at least two rows of chairs at curb side and perhaps as many as three or four rows of people standing behind them. Everyone was restless with excitement over the events surrounding the parade. Abe and I carefully slid between the crowd and walked across the empty street to Danny's. As we crossed the street and neared the entrance to the bar, Abe assumed a cocky swagger as he moved. He was somebody! There was to be no standing on the street curb for him. He boldly created a path through the line of people and we entered the bar. As my eyes adjusted to the dimly lit interior, I could see that other patrons of Danny's had chosen this as a refuge from the street and the sun as well. All of them seemed to be enjoying a drink or two while the festive atmosphere mounted on the streets.

Noticing that the seats nearest the windows were already filled up, I wondered if this confidence of Abe's was just another one of his disasters in the making. Yet, still, nothing seemed to be phasing Abe's mood of confidence and self-importance. We strolled on over to the bar and greeted Danny himself. Danny was a tall, slender and smiling red haired man in his late forties with large hands. Spread across the front of his apron were the ingredients of early morning Bloody Mary's. It was obvious he'd been busy. We both bought a six pack and Danny quietly said to Abe, "You fellas go right on up the back steps. That's reserved for my closest friends up there." I was impressed. It may not have been much, but I suddenly felt like somebody too.

We walked to the rear of the bar, past the kitchen and into a back storage room. Inside the storage room was another door which Abe opened. There it was, the rear stairway. A wide, dimly lit path of wood leading to the upper floor. Neighborhood legend said that, like Sladek's, this upper floor was once a dance hall. Now it was just a storage area rented by the hardware store next door. Plus, there was a collection of odd and broken bar furniture not being used anymore, a dust coated antique pinball machine, as well as old advertising signs from a prior era of tavern life—various beers and snack foods that had gone out of business.

Abe led the way through a maze of hardware boxes, bundles of bamboo rakes, coils of rope and so on. The plank floor was lit by a few bare light bulbs hanging loosely from the ceiling. Against the front wall were four tall double paned windows, each with its bottom half fully lifted. About ten men were gathered close to them. At the north window sat a large, fat man, in an old swivel chair with his large feet on the window sill. He was dressed in faded jeans and a loudly colored sport shirt. I recognized him as Benny Houdek, one of Abe's good pals.

"Hey Abe!" Benny hollered, "You guys can sit here. I saved this spot for ya."

Abe and I found an old double booth seat, dusted it off the best we could and dragged it next to Benny. As we each sat down and snapped open beers we could hear the drums from the lead band of the parade as they turned south off of Main Street. Within a few minutes we could see the Chippewa Harbor high school band in front of us. We all leaned out the window and watched. The sun gleamed and reflected off the gold trimmed uniforms and the brass instruments. Even though the band had already marched a couple miles, they still showed a disciplined formation and a pride in their performance.

The rest of the parade began to unfold behind the local high school band. Other bands were staggered throughout the rest of the parade and it began to seem that every high school band from Chippewa Harbor to Oshkosh was participating. There were three large convertibles following the lead band. Naturally, in the first, was the Fruit Grower's Festival Queen herself. While brandishing her gleaming and brilliantly white toothed smile, she waved to the crowd and we all politely clapped and waved back. "Some local darling whose life is not her own anymore," grunted Abe.

Seated in the second convertible were the mayor and three Chamber of Commerce, festival committee members. From the men at the large window next to us, I heard muffled, sarcastic remarks about this group. Being new to town I wasn't familiar with the Chamber yet. Convertible number three contained the State Governor and our local state Senator. They were proudly beaming and waving in a rather aggressive attempt to make contact with the crowd. From beside me, Benny leaned slightly out the open window and shouted, "This an election year, Gov?" As Benny leaned back in his chair he added, "You'd never see that damn fool around here otherwise."

From here on the parade seemed to become a conglomeration of local folksy things and glamorous kitsch. A truck passed by with a trailer carrying a polka band and a dancing couple. This was sponsored by Pobuda's Meat Market. Close behind was a float sponsored by the telephone company which was created out of crepe paper streamers and variously colored flowers. Pretty girls were placed on several levels and they waved and flashed phoney smiles. I thought to myself that this seemed like holdover moments from a pagan fertility festival or something. Soon, a troop of paunchy Legionaries struggled by, noticeably huffing and puffing for breath. This brought a loud guffaw from Benny and several others around me. Then came a long string of Queens from other local festivals: the Strawberry Queen, the Trout Queen, the Blueberry Queen and a whole host of others I can no longer remember.

While watching the variety of Queens go by I couldn't really tell if the motley cluster of men around me really enjoyed the parade or not. I sensed that the parade may have just been an excuse to participate in some late morning beer drinking. I think it was a bit of both. As the morning wore on and more beer was drunk the atmosphere became increasingly festive, but there also seemed to be undercurrents of humorous disdain and mockery as parade entries, like the Shriners, in their little circling cars, went by.

After a couple hours the last of the bands and floats passed beneath our vantage point of privilege. The parade watchers began to disband and mill around. The end came none too soon, I thought. The parade had become tedious. The small band of men I was with closed the big windows and began filing back through the maze of boxes and down the flight of stairs. As we emerged in the main lounge Abe suggested that we have a cold draught at the bar since we no longer had any of our own beer left. We just barely made it to the bar before the swell of new customers off the street began to fill every available space left in Danny's.

Danny was able to serve us before the supply of frosty mugs were all gone. The gulps of beer felt refreshing. As a newcomer to town I was curious about the local support for all the hoopla that had occurred over the last week of festivities. I knew that several of Benny's family were involved in the fruit growing business. I asked him in a rather business like fashion, "Benny, this week seems like a lot of craziness. Does any of it actually help the farmers?"

Benny moved his overweight body to face me and replied, in a matter of fact way, "Well, Jack, I'll tell ya, my Uncle Frank once said, he didn't make a red cent off the festival itself. Half the time his sweet cherries weren't even ripe. The festival people usually fly in a supply of cherries from Washington state or something. If his cherries were ripe, well, there was always some pocket change to be made at roadside stands. So to answer your question, the people making the real money are folks like Danny here, people in the restaurant and motel business, the small shops and all."

Benny had not seemed too pleased with the answer he had to give me. In fact, his rather negative feeling about the week's celebrations was something I was to encounter time and time again. When I finished my beer, I shook hands all around and left the others to continue their beery debates on local property taxes and the like.

This had been the summer of 1968. After I was married in 1969, Liz and I seldom watched any of the variety of festival events. They often seemed so silly—cherry pie eating contests, milk bottle regattas, pin the cherry on the tree kind of things. The parade became ho-hum to us except when we had an opportunity to watch from a second floor office building downtown while rejoicing with friends. Mostly, our local friends looked upon the festival as something to be endured for the sake of the summer economy. If one had the chance to leave town at this time, it was often taken.

As time passed, festivals came and went with a rather mundane regularity. Then suddenly, in the summer of 1982, a drastic and welcomed change occurred under the direction of Jim and Dale Willis. I had come to know these two brothers when they were students at Tamarack College. They were famous for walking around campus with devilish grins on their faces, as if a couple of jokers in a stack of playing cards. They held cult-style fame for their annual Halloween getups. If any tomfoolery occurred on school grounds they were usually at the bottom of it. Their closest friends claimed that it was nearly impossible to enjoy your food at the dinner table with these two because the constant stream of zany ideas they concocted left everyone, even parents, convulsed in laughter.

Through a subtle hint from one of my colleagues at the college, it was implied that I might not want to miss the parade this year as I had become accustomed to doing.

As the July day began, Liz and I did decide to attend the parade. We stood on the street, wondering and waiting. Nothing seemed any different. Certainly no one seemed aware of any secrets, or happenings. I wondered if I had been hearing things, maybe even being made a joke of myself.

The main body of the parade was gathered in the long, tree lined park in front of the old M&E

railroad depot. Floats, bands and other units that didn't fit underneath the shade of the park were lined up along Franklin Street to the east. Then, promptly, at ten a.m., the Chippewa Harbor high school band began marching and the 1982 Cherry Royale was under way. As the parade moved west on Main Street, the crowd at the curb responded with the usual polite clapping, cheers and smiles. No one noticed that, lurking in the alley by Mueller's Fish Market, were the Willis brothers. They had with them the greatest practical joke of their lives and were about to spring it on the town, the parade watchers and, of course, the unsuspecting Chamber of Commerce festival members.

Dale cautiously peered into the street looking for the right moment to enter the parade. About half way through the parade there appeared a gap between a high school band from southern Michigan and the next entry. Dale waved frantically and their mad project slid into place and began it's journey in the Cherry Royale. What the startled spectators saw was an old two-tone, aqua and white, Edsel convertible pulling a wagon of hay. On the wagon was a half pyramid of hay bales. Perched among the bales were six young women in gowns and cocktail dresses, each one had been appointed a Queen.

A large sign on the front of the hay wagon read, "National Hayfest." Perched higher than the others on the bales of hay sat the Hay Fever Queen herself, Anna Histemann from Kazund Heights, Ill.

One her attendants was The Refried Bean Queen, Miss Holly Pena from Heartburn, Arizona, the Visqueen, the Speed Queen and Miss Non-Dairy Products. All the Queens waved and smiled with a contrived phoniness. At intervals of about fifty feet, the wagon would come to a stop and everyone involved in the Hayfest would sneeze in unison. Nearby spectators roared their approval.

As this odd spectacle moved westward, the onlookers on the curbs, as well as those up in second story windows, would either break out in surprised laughter and point, or stand there, gawking, not knowing how to react, not knowing if this was real. The rousing marches that were being played by the bands continually drowned out each burst of laughter as the Hayfest moved along. The result was a slow moving wave of astonishment as each segment of the crowd was exposed to this wonder.

The Chamber of Commerce officials, who were the organizers of the parade, had chosen the second floor in a bank, on the corner of Main and Columbia streets, as their viewing spot. When the Willis Brothers creation reached the corner and made the left turn in front of the Chamber, most of them expressed surprise and a few, startled laughter. Most were incensed that the year of hard work they had put into this event was being trivialized by these upstarts in the Edsel convertible. The chairman of the parade committee frantically scanned the list of entries and found no mention of a Hayfest. These scalawags had sneaked in without the proper entry form. The nerve of them!

Outside the realm of the parade committee, however, the attitude was much different. It was unanimous amongst the people that the parade had become too stiff and rather tacky. The Willis brothers were instantly declared heroes by the people! Toasts and cheers for the Willis brothers were declared the rest of the day in popular locations such as Sladek's and Danny's!

Some members of the Chamber wanted to put an end to this sort of prank being performed again. However, it was clear that any move to suppress the Willis brothers would be bad public relations. Their parade entry had simply generated too much public approval. Word was sent forth to Jim and Dale that if they attempted to do this again, it would be appreciated if they might go through the proper channels and obtain an official entry form and procure a respectable sponsor.

As the summer wore on, the parade became a fleeting memory for most of the town. People returned to the tasks and chores of everyday life. Few realized that the Willis brothers had, in a figure of speech, tasted blood, and were quietly plotting the creation of a parade entry for the following year.

Sometime in late September of 1982, my wife received a phone call from Dale. He was inquiring if she would consider selling him her old Opel Kadet. When Liz asked my opinion, I gave an enthusiastic approval. I had been battling rust and corrosion on this car for three long years and was becoming weary trying to keep the body from complete disintegration with constant lacquerings of aluminium siding, rows of pop rivets, strips of duct tape and glops of roofing tar. Liz called Dale back and announced we would sell the Kadet and, if it was convenient, he could come by and take immediate possession.

When Dale arrived all of us realized that a price had not been established. Knowing the brothers appreciated the unorthodox, I blurted out, "Oh, how about a dollar?" Dale thought this was very funny as he groped around in his pockets for change, he ended up with one dollar and seven cents, we raised the price immediately. Dale handed all his change to Liz and then she asked, "Dale, what are you going to do with my little car?"

An impish grin came across Dale's face. He answered in a sly tone, between outbursts of laughter, "Oh hahaha, maybe you'll see next summer, hehehe. Just don't tell anyone about this, it must remain a secret, Ah-haha!"

Liz handed over the keys and the two of us swore to secrecy. As Dale got in the car to drive away we performed a mock marriage ceremony. Dale placed his left palm on the dashboard and I made him promise to love and to cherish the Kadet for the rest of his life. As he drove away, we were all chuckling.

The summer of 1983 was upon us before we knew it. A few days before the parade, Liz received another phone call from Dale asking if she would like to participate in this year's Cherry Royale. This was to be a reward for having sold him the Kadet at such an affordable price. My wife eagerly agreed to participate and was told to meet he and Jim at the float on Saturday. Liz asked how she'd find them.

"Oh Liz, hahaha, you won't miss it. Hahaha, just look down Franklin Street, I can hardly wait, hehehehe."

Liz did as she was instructed. What she found on Franklin Street, sandwiched between the variety of high school bands and other floats was a giant, thirty-four foot replica of a Hoover household vacuum cleaner, painted a brilliant blue and white. Jim spotted Liz when she arrived and proudly exclaimed, "The power source for this baby is none other than the Kadet Liz, hahaha ..."

The body of the vacuum was made from aluminium pipe with light canvas stretched over it. The vacuum bag was a long drape of canvas held up by a long pipe and hidden guy wires. The electric plug was strung out behind the vacuum and was made from a medium sized wastebasket. Liz was given, to her enthusiastic excitement, the task of carrying the "plug" alongside the Hoover. She was also to participate in various skits and ballyhoo with the other members of the float brigade the Willis brothers had put together.

The members of the marching bands close to the Willis entry, as well as other groups in the parade, stood still, gawking and marvelling at the vacuum cleaner. Bolder individuals approached for closer looks, some even laughed and complemented Dale and Jim on their marvelous invention. The more timid stood back and giggled from a safe distance.

As the parade began and each entry assumed proper formation, spectators on the street began to point and cheer, once again inspired by surprise. It was unanimous, the Willis brothers had struck gold again. The giant vacuum cleaner moved down Main Street giving off the sound of a real vacuum cleaner because of a loud cassette tape deep inside this monster machine. At the front of the vacuum were about twenty young women in white shorts, t-shirts and bright white caps. The t-shirts had been custom printed and identified the participants as the Hoover Hygienettes. Instead of twirling batons they twirled brooms and dustpans. The assorted people who picked up the rear of this daffy procession, perhaps seventy of them, were either shouldering push brooms like rifles, twirling feather dusters, or carrying trash cans. Every so often the cast of characters would flurry into action, dumping the contents of the trash cans and then proceed to clean things up.

The public was uproariously pleased. They were hooting and cheering and applauding this gigantic vacuum cleaner as a savior to the blandness of the Cherry Royale. In fact, the attendance at the parade was larger than ever in anticipation of another Willis brother prank. The parade committee was aware that the Willis brothers had brought more people out to the event this year, but they were still a bit agitated because of the way the entry form had been sent in. The form had been postmarked from Hooverville, Indiana and the entry had been entitled, "The Hooverville Drum and Bugle Corp." The entry had been accepted and thus given a respectable place in the parade. The committee had been fooled again!

Sadly, I was denied the opportunity to witness this grand event in person. I had been called to duty in my hometown. A minor crisis had occurred with my widowed mother. Upon my return Liz recounted the full range of excitement during the day. As I listened I was astonished and pleased. These brothers were heroes, their float and ideas were pure genius.

My first chance to see the infamous vacuum cleaner was at the end of October. I heard that the vacuum was to be brought out, and would be appearing at selected street corners on Halloween night. However, a day time test run was to occur at the old fairgrounds racetrack where the cleaner was being stored.

At the time, my dear cousin, Victor, was visiting from Germany and I felt certain that going to see this work of art would be of great interest to him too. It would be a classic example of American humor and inventiveness. Also, it would be an honor to have him take this story back to Germany with him. We were standing about thirty feet from the front of the old exhibition barn when the large wooden doors swung open and this marvelous creation appeared. There it stood, in all its creative force, the world's largest vacuum cleaner.

Somewhere inside this hulking giant was the fully cranked recording of a real household vacuum cleaner. As it began to slither along the wide gravel walkway to the fairgrounds racetrack I doubled, then tripled, then fell over in laughter. I cheered and clapped and yelled overwhelming praise. My theory of the creative energy that existed in Chippewa Harbor was vindicated right before my startled eyes.

My cousin Victor also seemed profoundly impressed. He was rocking back and forth in the grips of hearty laughter too. He began furiously taking photographs of the vacuum as we followed it around the small racetrack. I proudly told Victor that our Opel Kadet was the source of power. Victor suddenly turned to me and exclaimed.

"Ach, yes, Chack! In the Munich city, peebles vouldn't understand such humor. America is much funs!!" Yes, in those days, Chippewa Harbor was, "much funs!"

Unfortunately Chippewa Harbor is a city slowly homogenizing now, but Jim and Dale have held out. To this day they still conceal and place an entry in the parade each year. They have had a string of zany ideas, some of which have included the Weber Precision Grille Team, the Speed Queen featuring the world's longest clothesline as well as the Porta-Pasture featuring Miss Dairy-Aire and her Royal Quart.

The great Hoover appeared several more times in other city-wide festivals, always gaining praise and laughter wherever it went. The construction of this wonder placed the Willis brothers on another plateau. They were now considered to be artists and visionaries instead of pesky practical jokers and Halloween goblins. I have great admiration for these brothers. They are true visionaries and offer us all hope. They have brought the festival back to life in Chippewa Harbor and have enriched the place they live.

EPILOGUE

Working with Jack Ozegovic has been a blast. I call myself a coauthor "in spirit" as all of these stories are entirely, purely and joyfully his. I have merely had the privilege of winding around in, laughing with and exploring his adventures and memories. I am excited about sharing them with others.

During the creation of this book I was frequently asked why I wanted to work with these testaments to a land and subculture gone-by. My answer is in pursuit of hope. This is perhaps from the opposite end of Jack's desire to tell them. I believe he wants to save the memories of those he came to know and care about. He wants to stress the demise of the place he cherished and felt comfortable in.

The way the world changed around him and his friends in Michigan had to boil up deep feelings of angst, loss and rage. Certainly seeing what you care about being destroyed is infuriating and insulting. Developers, in team with the tourist industry, invaded his area of the world with a lack of respect for both tradition and place, as they most always do.

Despite all these problems, despite all these issues of change and disrespect I consider these stories to be rays of hope. When I ventured up to the Traverse City area for the first time I was greeted by many of Jack's friends who impressed me to no end. From vintners and mysterious cherry growers, to jokesters, teachers, artists, printing press makers, politicians, timber framers and others who seemed to know nothing but grand hospitality and idiosyncracy.

I met the son of one Jack's now deceased friends who wants to return to the area and make a life for himself. I imagine this inspiration to "return" is partly a tribute to his father's generation, but also because he recognizes a potential in the area, knows what his father and Jack and all their friends loved about the place. Not to believe in this region of the nation is to discount all those still living in the upper Midwest. It is to somehow suggest that the developers and "newcomers" have won. It is to discard all those who will find inspiration from this very book. Is to disregard everyone who sings *we shall overcome* ...

The people described in this book have never been a majority in our society and never will be, yet these people demonstrate the independence that will inspire me and others to follow our dreams. One can still choose to live in the land of the free and the brave. People of the minority have always figured out a way to live parallel with the sad bulk of the majority, alongside those involved with quests of emotional sterility, monetary greed, modem setting speeds, bland colored homes and superficial material goods. The tyrannical majority's pursuit of good is to be feared, never accepted. As author, farmer and fellow spirit seeker Gene Logsdon says, "More evil is done in the name of good than in any other fashion."

Finally, northwestern Michigan writer Jim Harrison once stated, "It only gradually occurred to me that our wounds are far less unique than our cures." I agree and believe this book is one of the cures.

Steve Semken
"Coauthor in Spirit"

The text of this book has been set in Adobe Garamond. The garamond typeface was designed by Jean Jannon in 1615. Garamond is characterized by little contrast between the thick and thin letter strokes, heavily bracketed serifs and oblique stress. The letterforms are open and round, making the face extremely readable.

This book is printed on 55# Glat, acid free, recycled, supple opaque, natural paper, meeting library standards.

Book printed by Thomson-Shore, Dexter, Michigan
Book Cover printed by Pinnacle Press, St. Louis, Missouri

Cover and book design assistance provided by
Laura Waldo and Jack Ozegovic

Printer's device designed by Andy Driscoll

Established in 1994, the Ice Cube Press is a small, independent press dedicated to publishing writing on nature, the environment and regionalism.

Also Available:
River Tips and Tree Trunks:
$14.95 ISBN 1-888160-63-2

Essays and meditations on the flow of water, the growth of trees and flight of the blue heron.

Moving With The Elements
$14.95 ISBN 1-888160-35-7

Stories, essays and weather reports on fire, water, earth and air, plus eccentric hearsay.

Coming soon to a town near you!
The Tin Prayer
Words From the Wild Testament
$7.95 ISBN 1-888160-01-2
Liturgy of the Wolverine

To order Ice Cube Press books
send checks or money orders to
(include $1.50 handling):

The Ice Cube Press & Letterpress
205 North Front Street
North Liberty, Iowa 52317-9302
write, or e-mail for more information
icecube@soli.inav.net
http://soli.inav.net/~icecube

Your patronage of this and all small, independent presses is appreciated.

As always, "Hear the other side"